Jobs for Youth
(Des emplois pour les jeunes)

Denmark 2010

OECD

ORGANISATION FOR ECONOMIC CO-OPERATION AND DEVELOPMENT

The OECD is a unique forum where the governments of 30 democracies work together to address the economic, social and environmental challenges of globalisation. The OECD is also at the forefront of efforts to understand and to help governments respond to new developments and concerns, such as corporate governance, the information economy and the challenges of an ageing population. The Organisation provides a setting where governments can compare policy experiences, seek answers to common problems, identify good practice and work to co-ordinate domestic and international policies.

The OECD member countries are: Australia, Austria, Belgium, Canada, the Czech Republic, Denmark, Finland, France, Germany, Greece, Hungary, Iceland, Ireland, Italy, Japan, Korea, Luxembourg, Mexico, the Netherlands, New Zealand, Norway, Poland, Portugal, the Slovak Republic, Spain, Sweden, Switzerland, Turkey, the United Kingdom and the United States. The Commission of the European Communities takes part in the work of the OECD.

OECD Publishing disseminates widely the results of the Organisation's statistics gathering and research on economic, social and environmental issues, as well as the conventions, guidelines and standards agreed by its members.

This work is published on the responsibility of the Secretary-General of the OECD. The opinions expressed and arguments employed herein do not necessarily reflect the official views of the Organisation or of the governments of its member countries.

ISBN 978-92-64-07515-3 (print)
ISBN 978-92-64-07516-0 (PDF)

ISSN 1997-6836 (print)
ISSN 1997-6844 (online)

Corrigenda to OECD publications may be found on line at: *www.oecd.org/publishing/corrigenda*.

FOREWORD

The OECD's Employment, Labour, and Social Affairs Committee has decided to carry out a thematic review of policies to facilitate the transition from school to work and improve the employment prospects of youth. This review is a key part of the implementation of the Reassessed OECD Jobs Strategy.

Sixteen countries (Australia, Belgium, Canada, Denmark, France, Greece, Japan, Korea, Netherlands, New Zealand, Norway, Poland, Slovak Republic, Spain, United Kingdom and United States) have decided to participate in this review, which began in 2006 and will be completed in 2010. Once all these countries have been reviewed, a synthesis report will be prepared highlighting the main issues and policy recommendations which will be discussed subsequently by the OECD Employment and Labour Ministers.

In this thematic review, the term youth encompasses "teenagers" (that is in statistical terms, youth aged 15/16-19), as well as "young adults" (aged 20-24 and 25-29).

This report on Denmark was prepared by Anne Sonnet (Project Leader), Chang-Hun Han and Vincent Vandenberghe, with the statistical assistance of Thomas Manfredi. It is the 15th such country report prepared in the context of this thematic review supervised by Stefano Scarpetta (Head of Division). A draft of this report was presented at a seminar held in Copenhagen on 8 September 2009. The seminar, which was organised by the Ministry of Employment, brought together representatives of the public authorities and social partners, as well as academic experts.

TABLE OF CONTENTS

Boxes

Figures

Tables

ACRONYMS

ALMP	Active Labour Market Programme
CV	Curriculum vitae (resume)
DKK	Danish kroner
EPL	Employment Protection Legislation
EU	European Union
EULFS	European Labour Force Survey
Eurostat	Statistical Office of the European Communities
EUSILC	European Survey on Income and Living Conditions
GDP	Gross Domestic Product
HILDA	Household, Income and Labour Dynamics in Australia Survey
ILO	International Labour Organisation
ISCED	International Standard Classification of Education
LIFO	Last-in first-out
LTU	Long-term Unemployment
NEET	Neither in employment nor education or training
PES	Public Employment Service
PISA	OECD's Programme for International Student Assessment
SA	Social assistance
UIB	Unemployment insurance benefits
UR	Unemployment rate
VET	Vocational education and training system
YAP	Youth Allowance Programme
YUP	Youth Unemployment Programme

SUMMARY AND MAIN RECOMMENDATIONS

Denmark has a dynamic youth labour market outperforming most OECD countries but is challenged by the current jobs crisis

The current economic downturn has brought about a worsening in the labour market performance of Danish youth. In the year to the third quarter 2009, the unemployment rate of youth aged 15-24 rose by 2.7 percentage points to 11.4% according to the labour force survey. However, the youth unemployment rate in Denmark is still well below the corresponding OECD average (17.6%) and even below the levels observed in many other OECD countries before the crisis.

Denmark entered this global economic crisis with rather favourable labour market conditions. In particular, the youth employment rate was very high from an international perspective: in 2008, it reached a high point at 68.5%, 25 percentage points above the corresponding OECD average.

Moreover, the transition from school to work is traditionally very smooth for most Danish youth. Many enter the job market when they are still studying and the time it takes for school-leavers to find their first job is usually short. In addition, the gap between youth with and without an upper secondary education in terms of time to find their first job was, in 2008, smaller than in most of other OECD countries, partly because of the tight labour market. There is however some evidence that in Denmark, the labour market performance of children of immigrants is less satisfactory than the one of children of natives.

Denmark has a well-developed institutional and policy setting that allows most of youth to get a firm foothold in the labour market. This setting will help them weather the current jobs crisis better than in many other OECD countries and prepare them for the recovery. Number of the schemes that other OECD countries are hastily introducing to cope with the immediate consequences of the crisis were already available in Denmark before the current downturn.

In particular, young individuals in Denmark are insured against the risk of poverty by a combination of generous unemployment insurance and social assistance benefits. An elaborate set of rules, derived from the "mutual obligations" principle, activate financially-assisted youth to find a job, if they are job-ready, and to complete their education, if they are without an upper secondary education. Moreover, in Denmark, public funding for active labour market programmes (ALMPs) is automatically adjusted according to the government's official unemployment forecasts to ensure sufficient resources to support the larger number of jobless persons, including youth.

These underlying institutional features imply that youth in Denmark potentially face a lower risk of long-term unemployment, poverty and exclusion than in other OECD countries during the economic downturn. In this respect, there is a limited risk of a "lost generation" (like in Japan in the 1990s) created by a prolonged disengagement of youth from the labour market and the associated human capital depreciation. At the same time, the Danish model is also better placed to promote a rapid reintegration of youth into employment once economic growth picks up again.

The tentative conclusion is that the Danish government can focus more on the supposedly less challenging tasks of improving its existing schemes and evaluating their capacity to combat rising youth unemployment, instead of putting in place new programmes, as is the case in a number of other OECD countries.

Recent initiatives to tackle youth unemployment

Despite these strengths of the youth labour market in Denmark, like in other OECD countries, some youth are particularly hard hit by the current economic downturn. For example, recruitment of apprentices by Danish firms fell by 24% in the first eight months of 2009, compared with the same period in 2008. Many tertiary studies require students to complete a compulsory work placement and it is feared that, if students do not secure one, they will drop out of their studies. The Danish government has therefore announced in September 2009 that it will invest DKK 1.3 billion (approximately EUR 180 million) in securing 5 000 new apprenticeship and training places next year: 1 650 places in private companies; 1 500 places in schools offering programmes targeted on occupations facing skill shortages; 1 650 places in regions and municipalities; and 200 places in public administration.

In addition, in November 2009 the government and the three major political parties have agreed on a series of policies designed to ensure a quick, intensive and focused approach towards youth aged 15-17, 18-19 and 18-29. These actions cover both the Ministry of Education and the Ministry of Employment.

Concerning the 15-17-year-olds, all pupils in lower secondary education will prepare an education plan in collaboration with their parents, the school and the youth guidance centre (the institution that has primary responsibility for initiatives in relation to the individuals under the age of 18). The education plan should lead to further education or describe what the young person will otherwise be doing and may include activities such as training, employment, internship, stay abroad or volunteer work. If pupils do not follow their education plan, their parents will risk losing child benefits. Additional resources have been provided for increased co-operation between youth guidance centres, educational institutions and the Public Employment Service (PES). The Ministry of Education and the Ministry of Employment will co-operate to develop a database, which will ensure a full overview of the education and training of each young individual. This will enable a quick identification of vulnerable young people and provide the information needed to offer a targeted effort.

Initiatives targeted at the 18-19-year-olds focus on a package offering intensive contact with the PES and rapid activation. The package includes an individual interview after only one week of applying for welfare benefits, a job-search training course within the first two weeks and an active measure (an educational opportunity or work placement) offered no later than one month after the beginning of the unemployment period.

More generally for all youth aged 18-30, the aim is to tackle long-term unemployment. In particular, the PES will propose a hiring subsidy in the private sector for young people under 30 who have been recipients of welfare benefits for longer than 12 months. In addition, young people without qualifications will take a reading and writing test when they register as unemployed and the PES has been given resources to provide literacy and numeracy courses. The PES will also be obliged to refer new graduates under 30 to a private provider after only six weeks of unemployment (previously after 4-7 months depending on the level of education).

Suggested recommendations in response to the remaining challenges

The recent initiatives go in the right direction to prevent youth most at risk from dropping out of school and to maintain contact with the labour market during the downturn. However, their implementation should be carefully monitored to adapt them as necessary and/or to scale them up to address the structural challenges facing the youth labour market in Denmark. In particular, the Danish government should focus on three areas: *i)* ensuring that everyone leaving education is capable of gaining the skills needed on the labour market; *ii)* removing remaining demand-side barriers to promote better jobs for more youth; and *iii)* strengthening activation to better help disadvantaged youth.

Ensuring that everyone leaving education is capable of gaining the skills needed on the labour market

Disappointing PISA test scores

Test scores from the OECD Programme for International Student Assessment (PISA) 2003 and 2006 reveal, on average, a mixed performance for Danes at age 15. In particular, Danish teenagers perform at the OECD average level in mathematics and slightly below the OECD average in reading, despite Denmark's relatively high GDP per capita and, especially the very generous public funding on education, which amounted 4.4% of the GDP in 2006 (well above the OECD average of 3.7%).[1]

These somewhat disappointing results should encourage the Danish authorities to further strengthen the curriculum in primary and lower secondary schools. Extensive reforms are currently being implemented in the primary and lower secondary schools with the aim of improving the level of attainment in particular in reading literacy, science and mathematics.

The government has established in 2006 a new national agency for quality assurance and evaluation in primary and lower secondary schools and in the same year, the Danish Parliament decided to make national tests a compulsory pedagogic tool in primary and lower secondary schools. The main purpose of the Danish National Test Reform is to provide teachers with a pedagogical tool which can help them analyse the proficiency level of their pupils and the level of their class. This is a step in the right direction. Standardised tests create an environment in which schools, teachers and municipalities pay more attention to the determinants of children's school attainment.

But Denmark has theoretically banned any form of ranking of schools based on test scores. There are a number of reasons for preventing individual raw scores to be disseminated. In particular, raw score gaps tend to reflect not only teaching quality differentials but also differences in socioeconomic background factors that can influence pupils' performance. However, Denmark's very restrictive approach of results dissemination may weaken incentives for improvements, as poor performance receives little publicity. Moreover, the scheme contains no element of school accountability as there are no consequences attached to poor school performance. It thus remains to be seen whether Denmark's policy of "soft testing" will be an effective mean of bringing the expected changes to schools' performance.

---

1.   Education includes primary, secondary and post-secondary non-tertiary education.

A higher than expected school drop-out rate in general

Denmark is also characterised by a relatively high school drop-out rate. The proportion of those aged 20-24 who did not complete upper secondary school was 15.6% in 2008, slightly below the OECD average of 16% but well above the corresponding rate recorded in central European countries or other Nordic countries like Sweden (9%) or Finland (9.7%). Recognising this poor school outcome, the Danish government is currently committed to ensure that 95% of each youth cohort should complete upper secondary education in 2015, although reaching that target will prove difficult to achieve from the level of 83% in 2007.

Denmark's relatively high drop-out rate seems to be partially driven by the relative inability of the basic education system to equip disadvantaged youth with core literacy and numeracy skills. In particular, PISA has demonstrated lower assessment results for the children of immigrants in Denmark and there are close links between poor PISA outcomes and high drop-out rates.

The VET system performs well for those who complete it

By contrast, Denmark has a good vocational education and training (VET) system for those aged 16 and more. The Danish VET system is relatively demanding. It takes on average four years to obtain a VET degree. Research also suggests that a good level of mathematics is the best passport to success in some VET programmes. An important aspect of VET in Denmark is its strong "dual" component, synonymous with: *i)* systematic involvement of firms and social partners; and *ii)* (partially as a result of that) a high job-readiness for those who complete it.

However, access to VET intervenes late, typically after the end of compulsory education (16 years of age) and the traditional gap years that young Danes grant themselves before undertaking an upper secondary qualification. The latter explains in great part why in 2005 the average age of all students starting VET was almost 21.

The drop-out rate in VET is high, in particular among immigrant youth of non-western origin. Admittance in the "basic course", the school part of VET, is free for all young people who have completed nine years of elementary school. Entering the dual part of a VET programme after the basic course, the so-called "main course", is more difficult since the apprentice must have found a contract with a firm to apply for it. It is almost entirely up to the students to find a firm willing to take them as apprentices. When they do not find an apprenticeship contract in a specific VET programme, many of them are able to find one in another VET programme or continue in general upper secondary education programmes. Nonetheless,

40% of all VET drop-outs are estimated not to continue any education or training programme.

Apprentice wages have a special regime. Within each sector, a minimum wage for apprentices is negotiated every third year in collective labour agreements. Additionally, the apprentice – as in an ordinary employment contract – has the opportunity to negotiate a higher salary. Firms receive important subsidies to hire and train apprentices. As a result, the average cost for an apprentice is half the cost for an ordinary employee. The wage received by an apprentice is however attractive for a young person, being on average 60% higher than the state education grant.

Reducing VET's drop-out rate while preserving the quality of VET students

Policy makers, rightly concerned by the overall incidence of drop-outs, are trying to improve the quality of VET (*e.g.* mandatory action plans within VET schools and mentoring). They are also reforming VET in order to accommodate the needs of those forming the lower end of the skill distribution (shorter programmes leading to partial qualifications, or less school-based education implying fewer weeks sitting in school before starting apprenticeship within firms). The challenge, however, is to raise VET attendance and completion rates without compromising quality, in particular the willingness of firms to recruit, train and pay apprentices.

Probably the oldest students in the OECD

Denmark probably has among the oldest students and graduates in the OECD, meaning that – unless Danes effectively retire later[2] – they spend fewer years in employment. Some argue that older students in Denmark have accumulated significant labour market experience as many of them hold student jobs, something that help them have a smoother and faster transition into stable employment. Indeed, in 2008, about 70% of students aged 23-24 were working. Yet, even more Australian students (78%), for example, work at the same age but still manage on average to graduate at a much younger age.

The delay in completing education starts at the end of compulsory education. Students very often take the voluntary 10th grade[3] in the

---

2.   The employment rate of workers aged 55-64 in 2008 in Denmark was effectively above the corresponding rate in OECD and in the European Union (respectively 58%, 54% and 47%).

3.   The 10th grade was conceived as an opportunity for less able students to catch up on material not learnt well during the nine compulsory years of schooling and clarify their choice of upper secondary education.

compulsory school system, even if they are academically ready for further education. There are thus long waits between the lower secondary and the upper secondary cycles. A similar phenomenon is observed at the articulation between upper secondary education and tertiary education. Moreover, within tertiary education, Danish students frequently change study course, implying that they are older when they start the programme they eventually graduate from.

Addressing this issue is challenging as there is no straightforward answer to a phenomenon that is deeply rooted in the Danish culture. Possible options include: *i)* a better command of core skills at the end of compulsory education in order to increase the level of "study readiness" of teenagers; *ii)* improved guidance within schools; and *iii)* a well-designed set of financial incentives rewarding early start and completion of tertiary education.

In the 2006 Welfare Agreement, a number of measures were announced to combat the late-study-completion syndrome. The single most important change consisted of making access to tertiary education easier if the student does not wait more than two years after completing upper secondary education. Under the new setting, the prospective students have their grade average multiplied by 1.08, implying an easier access to studies where the number of places is limited by a *numerus clausus*. However, the odds are that this is unlikely to significantly affect students' behaviour as open access exists to most study programmes.

Measures aimed at changing the attitude of providers *(i.e.* tertiary education institutions) were also announced in the Welfare Agreement. In particular, new financing structures should bring the actual study duration better in line with the scheduled one. The intention was also that part of the public financing should be paid out to providers only when students complete the exams. The final report of the 2007 Labour Market Commission[4] also proposed a range of measures to encourage earlier completion of education.

These are steps in the right direction. But other decisions could prove counterproductive. For instance the decision to increase earnings ceilings for students allow them to earn more while still receiving full education grants and may indeed delay study completion. Research finds that the higher the student's own earnings, the longer it takes to complete studies. It is noteworthy that the Swedish Fiscal Policy Council has just recommended

---

4.   The Labour Market Commission was established in 2007 to provide recommendations on how to achieve the employment goals required by the government's 2015 Plan for fiscal policy and released its final report in August 2009.

reducing the earnings limit so as to encourage students to work less and focus on their studies.

To ensure that all youth have the basic skills needed to enter, and progress, on the labour market and are enticed to rapidly put them to use, the following measures could be envisaged:

- *In primary and lower-secondary education, enhance the National Test Reform and make sure schools are more accountable.* There is international evidence that externally-defined standards such as those set out in the 2006-enacted National Test Reform help combat the tendency of teachers to lower expectations and demands when confronted with presumably low-skilled pupils. If there are good reasons for preventing individual raw scores to be disseminated, Denmark's decision to strictly confine school ranking based on test scores should be reconsidered. In addition, elements of school accountability, based on verifiable outcomes (*e.g.* pupils' progress in core topics), should be developed.

- *Tackle the high drop-out rate in VET programmes.* Teenagers should be better prepared before starting the basic course of a VET programme. Offering more opportunities to participate in practical work in "production" schools[5] could be a possibility as well as a better individual monitoring in primary and lower secondary education. Youth guidance centres should better assist young people when they apply for the main course and are seeking for an apprenticeship in a firm. It is important that the PES and youth guidance centres co-operate closely to find more apprenticeship places.

- *Invest in a fully-fledged activation strategy aimed at reducing the overall time to graduation.* The combination of high income tax and generous education grants creates adverse incentives to take extended breaks between upper secondary and tertiary education and to prolong studies once started. Since altering the current high income tax/generous student financing mix may be difficult to envisage, Denmark needs to develop an ambitious activation strategy[6] targeting students but also educational institutions, with the

---

5. Since 1978, these schools offer youth aged 16 or more who are not ready for the normal VET programme the opportunity to participate in practical work in different areas ranging from metal, carpentry and textiles to media, theatre and music.

6. Replicating in the sense the philosophy that Denmark implemented very successfully for welfare benefits.

explicit aim of enticing both sides to foster students to start and complete education on time. As part of this strategy, adjustments should be made to student grants rewarding early entry and on-schedule completion of studies. Simultaneously, full-rate taximeters[7] financing tertiary education institutions should only be available for those that recruit and graduate on-schedule students.

Removing remaining demand-side barriers to promote better jobs for more youth

Until mid-2008, Denmark was characterised by a very tight labour market. Capacity utilisation rose close to historical peaks and skilled labour shortages became a more prominent constraint. A tight labour market also implied more employment opportunities for low-educated workers or for immigrants.

The short-term policy challenges posed by the recession

The current economic downturn is challenging some of the very good labour market outcomes in Denmark. The first reaction of firms to a sharp economic slowdown is to cease hiring before commencing on the more expensive procedure of redundancies. It is evident that young people comprise a disproportionate segment of job seekers and are thus more heavily affected by a freeze in new recruitments.

The cost to firms of firing young workers is also generally lower than for prime-age workers. Being less experimented than the latter, young workers involve a smaller loss of specific know-how to firms making them redundant. Moreover, young workers have lower tenure and are often involved in temporary jobs. Both factors reduce the dismissal costs for their employers and youth are often the first to go during downturns: an illustration of the last-in first-out (LIFO) phenomenon.

However, it is worth stressing that in Denmark there are no differences in the degree of employment protection provided by legislation or regulations between young and older workers.[8] This is the consequence of Denmark's tradition of labour market flexibility as part of the "flexicurity" model, whereby private sector employees can be easily dismissed. Other things being equal, it implies that the overall cost of the economic crisis in terms of job destructions should be less concentrated on young workers than in other OECD countries. Besides a relatively lax employment protection

---

7.   The Danish version of the voucher system.

8.   This is the case for example in Spain, Poland or France.

legislation framework, Denmark has also a moderate tax-wedge by western European standards.

But it may still make sense to try to compensate for the disadvantage youth tend to suffer from when labour demand falters. A way to achieve that goal consists of making especially at-risk youth more attractive for private employers *via* temporary and targeted reductions in labour costs.

To better cope with the current crisis and tackle the remaining demand-side barriers to youth employment, the following measures should be considered:

- *In a period of faltering labour demand, social partners should explore ways of temporary reducing the cost of employing low-skilled youth.* In practice, this could be done by extending to all school drop-outs below the age of, say, 25 the wage regime that sectors/firms currently apply to VET apprentices. This would raise the degree of income differentiation across educational groups and the incentives to invest in human capital: something supposedly helpful in reducing the incidence of school drop-out. Such a measure should be evaluated after a short period of implementation in order to decide whether it should be removed once the recovery is back.

- *Alternatively, the same effect on the youth labour demand could be achieved by more generous hiring subsidies in the private sector for disadvantaged youth.* Very recently, the Danish government announced such hiring subsidies for youth who have been recipients of welfare benefits for longer than 12 months. Such a measure should be evaluated after a certain time to ensure that it is cost-effective and to decide whether it could become a long-term policy.

Strengthening activation to better help all disadvantaged youth

Generous welfare benefits coupled to activation measures

Unemployed young people in Denmark are covered by one of the most generous income-support system in the OECD area. The net replacement rate provided by unemployment insurance benefits is among the highest in OECD, and the maximum benefit duration of four years is also one of the longest. Means-tested[9] social assistance is also generous by international standards and available for all those who do not (or no longer) qualify for unemployment insurance benefits as from the age of 18.

While relatively generous welfare schemes theoretically bear the risk of creating unemployment and inactivity traps, in Denmark activation measures

---

9.   Social assistance in Denmark is means-tested on family income and wealth.

targeted at youth successfully promote their rapid reintegration in employment. As already mentioned, this is a result of a strict and well-established implementation of the "mutual obligations" activation approach introduced in the mid-1990s whereby, in exchange for income support, job seekers (including youth) need to participate in training, job-search or placement activities (the flexicurity approach). There are benefit sanctions for refusing to participate.

During the second part of the 1990s and in the early 2000s, activation was fine-tuned and reinforced, especially in relation to youth, with apparent success. Before the onset of the economic crisis, the incidence of long-term youth unemployment was extremely low in Denmark by international standards. In 2008, it represented 6.4% of youth unemployment, compared with 23.9% and 18.8% in, respectively, the European Union and the OECD.

From August 2009, the PES is further decentralised and the implementation of ALMPs is the responsibility of municipalities. This removes the previous distinction between national offices, administering benefits for insured unemployed people, and local offices, administering benefits for social welfare recipients – all unemployed will now be dealt with by the same agency (one-stop shop) in each municipality. However, this new arrangement raises the risk of increased diversity in the services offered between different municipalities, although measures have been put in place to monitor consistency with national employment policies. It is important that the decentralisation process is carefully assessed as from the beginning to ensure that effective services are delivered to youth in particular.

Early intervention and six months of activation for all benefit recipients below the age of 30

From the summer of 2009, after a first interview between one month (previously three) and a maximum of three months (previously six) of unemployment, all youth under 30 receiving unemployment insurance or social assistance benefits must take part in activation programmes lasting six months. Activation rules are the strictest for youth under 25 without an upper secondary qualification and without children. They are obliged to enroll in an educational programme, either in the ordinary educational system if they are ready or otherwise in a special education programme to prepare them for ordinary education. By contrast, all types of ALMPs can be used for youth aged 25-29 and for youth with children.

Furthermore, since 1996, with the enactment of the Youth Unemployment Programme (YUP), youth aged 18-24 without an upper secondary educational attainment already saw their level of unemployment benefits cut by 50% (close to the level of the education grant) after six months in unemployment and were obliged to enter a special education programme. A benefit reduction after six months of activation was progressively extended to all youth under 25 receiving welfare benefits. However, for recipients aged 25-29 and for all youth with children, the welfare benefit is not reduced, even if they have a low educational attainment. And there is evidence that these groups tend to stay longer on welfare benefits also because of their weaker incentives to move quickly into employment.

Threat effect versus programme effect?

Back in the 1980s, two components of the so-called "flexicurity" model – flexible employment regulations and generous welfare benefits – were already part of the Danish labour market landscape, but unemployment rates were high, particularly for youth. Their potential effects on the duration of unemployment were significantly strengthened by stricter enforcement of job search eligibility conditions and reinforced re-employment strategies, important elements of the so-called activation strategy.

But activation policies are costly. Given the extensive use of these policies in Denmark, it is not surprising that public expenditure on ALMPs[10] (1% of GDP in 2007) is well above the OECD average (0.4% of GDP) and among the highest in OECD countries. Various studies find strong threat effects of activation policies, whereas the evidence on the effects of individual ALMPs is mixed.

Push to employment or back to education?

Many ALMPs in the OECD have historically been developed around a work-for-the-dole philosophy. But during the present downturn, a shift from a "work-first" to a "skill-first" strategy – which prioritises education and training over immediate job placement – is visible in a number of OECD countries for disadvantaged youth. In Denmark, the YUP for example already had a clear positive effect on the transition rate into education, whereas the effect on the immediate transition into employment was more uncertain. The international evidence shows that a work-first activation strategy works better for skilled youth who are job-ready, but a skill-first activation strategy is more relevant for disadvantaged youth who often lack the skills needed on the labour market. A shift to a skill-first activation strategy during the current downturn might help low-skilled youth to be better equipped for the recovery.

The following measures could be envisaged to improve the effectiveness of Denmark's welfare system in relation to youth:

---

10.   Excluding PES and administration.

- *Extent stronger financial incentives in moving out of welfare benefits to low-educated youth aged 25-29.* Some Danish analysts and the Labour Market Commission have recommended the extension of stricter welfare benefits rules up to the age of 30. This reform should be implemented swiftly. However, young parents *a priori* should not be considered as a group that could be exempted from the mainstream activation strategy.

- *Make sure that the skill-upgrading services offered are tailored to the profiles of jobless youth and in particular to school drop-outs resuming education.* There is now a growing need to put more emphasis on skill-upgrading activities and a shift to a skill-first strategy should be considered for the most disadvantaged youth. For disengaged youth, it is important to avoid the back-to-the-classroom option as the latter might prove very counterproductive. Danish evaluation suggests that only training programmes with a strong on-the-job component have a positive effect on post-programme employment and wage prospects. The priority should be put on programmes taught outside traditional schools with regular exposure to work experience, preferably under the umbrella of organisations that have been historically involved in job placement or counselling.

- *Develop a residential option as part of the arsenal of measures aimed at helping very disadvantaged youths.* Standard ALMPs are unlikely to work for the most disadvantaged youths who usually cumulate social risk factors (low education, ethnic minority background, drug use, mental illness, etc.). For this group, more radical and costly options are probably needed. One possibility – using the existing "production" schools and Folk High Schools[11] as platforms – would be to systematise the offering of a boarding-school type environment, delivering a mix of: *i)* adult mentoring; *ii)* work/production experience; and *iii)* remedial education. Models for this initiative could come from the long-standing US Job Corps programme.

---

11.   Education residential programmes where traditional Nordic life skills are taught without any recognised diploma.

RÉSUMÉ ET PRINCIPALES RECOMMANDATIONS

Le marché du travail des jeunes au Danemark est dynamique et plus performant que dans la plupart des pays de l'OCDE mais doit faire face aux défis de la crise actuelle de l'emploi

Face au ralentissement économique actuel, la situation des jeunes Danois sur le marché du travail s'est aggravée. Entre les troisièmes trimestres 2008 et 2009, le taux de chômage des jeunes de 15 à 24 ans a augmenté de 2.7 points de pourcentage pour s'établir à 11.4 % selon l'Enquête sur les forces de travail. Cependant, le taux de chômage des jeunes au Danemark est encore nettement plus bas que le taux moyen correspondant dans la zone de l'OCDE (17.6 %) et même que les taux observés dans de nombreux pays de l'OCDE avant la crise.

Lorsque le Danemark est entré dans cette crise économique mondiale, la situation de son marché du travail était assez favorable. En particulier, le taux d'emploi des jeunes y était très élevé comparé à celui des autres pays de l'OCDE : en 2008, il atteignait 68.5 %, soit 25 points de pourcentage au-dessus de la moyenne OCDE correspondante.

De plus, la transition de l'école à l'emploi s'effectue aussi de manière très harmonieuse pour la plupart des jeunes Danois. Beaucoup entrent dans la vie active alors qu'ils sont encore étudiants et le délai nécessaire pour trouver un emploi à la sortie des études est court lui aussi. De plus, en termes du temps nécessaire pour trouver le premier emploi, l'écart entre les jeunes ayant terminé le deuxième cycle de l'enseignement secondaire et ceux ayant décroché avant était, en 2008, inférieur à l'écart relevé dans la plupart des autres pays de l'OCDE, en partie parce que le marché du travail était tendu. Pour autant, il apparaît qu'au Danemark, les performances sur le marché du travail des enfants d'immigrés sont moins satisfaisantes que celles des enfants de parents danois.

Le Danemark s'est doté d'un cadre institutionnel et de réglementation bien élaboré qui permet à de nombreux jeunes de s'insérer durablement sur le marché du travail. Ce cadre sera à même de les aider à éprouver moins de difficultés à surmonter la crise actuelle de l'emploi que leurs homologues de beaucoup d'autres pays de l'OCDE, tout en les préparant à la reprise. Nombre de dispositifs mis en place à la hâte par d'autres pays de l'OCDE pour faire face aux conséquences immédiates de la crise existaient déjà au Danemark avant le ralentissement actuel.

C'est ainsi qu'au Danemark les jeunes sont assurés contre le risque de pauvreté par un généreux système de prestations conjuguant assurance chômage et aide sociale. Un ensemble de règles complexes dérivées du principe des « obligations réciproques » encourage activement les jeunes bénéficiant d'allocations sociales à rechercher un emploi, s'ils sont prêts à en occuper un ou à terminer leurs études, s'ils n'ont pas de diplôme équivalent au deuxième cycle du secondaire. De surcroît, au Danemark, le budget public affecté aux programmes actifs du marché du travail est réajusté automatiquement en fonction des prévisions officielles de chômage. L'État s'assure ainsi de disposer de ressources suffisantes pour aider les demandeurs d'emploi, y compris les jeunes, dès l'instant où leur nombre augmente.

Ces dispositifs ancrés dans les institutions font qu'au Danemark, les jeunes ont probablement moins de risques de connaître le chômage de longue durée, la pauvreté ou l'exclusion que leurs homologues des autres pays de l'OCDE en cette période de ralentissement économique. A cet égard, le risque est limité de voir se constituer une « génération sacrifiée » (à l'image de ce que le Japon a connu dans les années 90) liée au retrait prolongé des jeunes du marché du travail et à l'appauvrissement du capital humain que cela engendre. En même temps, le modèle danois est bien placé pour favoriser le retour rapide à l'emploi des jeunes une fois que la croissance économique sera réamorcée.

Les premières conclusions sont que le gouvernement danois pourrait se concentrer davantage sur la mission *a priori* moins exigeante consistant à améliorer les dispositifs qu'il a mis en place, et à évaluer leur capacité à lutter contre le chômage croissant des jeunes au lieu de mettre en place de nouveaux programmes comme c'est le cas dans un certain nombre d'autres pays de l'OCDE.

Initiatives récentes pour faire face au chômage des jeunes

Malgré les atouts du marché du travail des jeunes au Danemark, comme dans les autres pays de l'OCDE, certains jeunes sont plus fortement touchés dans la crise économique actuelle. Par exemple, le recrutement d'apprentis par des firmes danoises a diminué de 24 % au cours des huit premiers mois de 2009 comparés à la même période de 2008. De nombreuses formations supérieures exigent que les étudiants fassent un stage obligatoire et il est à craindre que si les étudiants ne trouvent pas de place de stage, ils ne pourront pas terminer leurs études. C'est pourquoi le gouvernement danois a annoncé en septembre 2009 qu'il investira 1.3 milliards DKK (environ 180 millions EUR) pour garantir 5 000 nouvelles places d'apprentissage et de stage pour l'année prochaine ; 1 650 places dans des entreprises privées ; 1 500 places dans des écoles offrant des programmes ciblés sur des qualifications en pénurie; 1 650 places dans les régions et communes ; et 200 places dans l'administration publique.

De plus en novembre 2009, le gouvernement et les trois principaux partis politiques ont convenu d'une série de mesures de soutien rapide, intensif et ciblé sur les jeunes de 15-17 ans, de 18-19 ans et plus globalement sur tous les jeunes de 18-29 ans. Ces actions concernent à la fois le ministère de l'Éducation et celui de l'Emploi.

Concernant les 15-17 ans, tous les élèves du cycle inférieur du secondaire vont préparer un plan d'éducation en collaboration avec leurs parents, l'école et le centre d'orientation pour les jeunes (l'institution qui est responsable en premier chef des mesures pour les jeunes de moins de 18 ans). Le plan d'éducation devrait conduire à la poursuite des études ou décrire ce que le jeune va faire, et peut inclure les actions suivantes : se former, travailler, faire un stage, passer du temps à l'étranger ou s'engager comme volontaire. Si les élèves ne suivent pas leur plan d'éducation, leurs parents risquent de perdre leurs allocations familiales. Des ressources additionnelles ont été apportées pour intensifier la coopération entre les centres d'orientation pour les jeunes, les institutions éducatives et le service public de l'emploi (SPE). Le ministère de l'Éducation et celui de l'Emploi vont développer conjointement une base de données qui apportera une vue d'ensemble sur le niveau d'instruction et de formation de chaque jeune. Cela permettra d'identifier rapidement les jeunes vulnérables et fournira l'information nécessaire pour mettre en œuvre une intervention ciblée.

Les initiatives ciblées sur les 18-19 ans portent sur un ensemble de mesures intensifiant les contacts avec le SPE et une activation rapide. Ces mesures comprennent un entretien individuel dans la semaine qui suit la demande d'allocations sociales, un cours d'aide à la recherche d'emploi durant les deux premières semaines et l'offre d'une mesure active (une opportunité d'études ou de travail) dans le mois qui suit le début de la période de chômage.

Plus largement, pour l'ensemble des jeunes de 18 à 29 ans, le but est de s'attaquer au chômage de longue durée. En particulier, le SPE proposera une subvention à l'embauche dans le secteur privé pour les jeunes de moins de 30 ans qui sont bénéficiaires d'une aide sociale depuis plus de 12 mois. De plus, les jeunes sans qualification passeront un test de lecture et d'écriture au moment de leur inscription au chômage et le SPE a été doté de moyens financiers pour leur offrir des cours de compréhension de l'écrit et de mathématiques. Le SPE sera également tenu d'envoyer les nouveaux diplômés de moins de 30 ans auprès d'un prestataire privé dès six semaines de chômage (auparavant dès quatre à sept mois selon le niveau de diplôme).

Recommandations suggérées pour répondre aux défis actuels

Ces initiatives récentes vont dans la bonne direction pour empêcher le décrochage scolaire dans le groupe des jeunes les plus à risque et pour les maintenir en contact avec le marché du travail pendant le ralentissement économique. Cependant, leur mise en œuvre devrait être étroitement suivie pour les adapter si nécessaire et/ou les renforcer pour faire face aux défis structurels du marché du travail des jeunes Danois. Plus précisément, le gouvernement danois devrait concentrer son action sur trois domaines : *i)* veiller à ce que chacun, à la sortie du système d'enseignement, soit capable d'acquérir les compétences nécessaires sur le marché du travail ; *ii)* s'attaquer aux barrières qui existent du côté de la demande pour promouvoir de meilleurs emplois pour plus de jeunes ; et *iii)* renforcer l'activation pour mieux aider les jeunes défavorisés.

Veiller à ce que chacun, à la sortie du système d'enseignement, soit capable d'acquérir les compétences nécessaires sur le marché du travail

Des résultats décevants aux tests PISA

Les notes obtenues par les élèves lors des tests passés en 2003 et 2006 dans le cadre du Programme international pour le suivi des acquis des élèves (PISA) de l'OCDE révèlent qu'en moyenne, les Danois âgés de 15 ans obtiennent des résultats mitigés. En particulier, les adolescents au Danemark ont des performances correspondant à la moyenne de l'OCDE en mathématiques, mais légèrement inférieures à cette même moyenne en compréhension de l'écrit et ce, malgré le PIB par habitant relativement élevé du Danemark et, surtout l'extrême générosité du financement public de l'éducation[12], qui atteignait 4.4 % du PIB en 2006 (chiffre très au-dessus de la moyenne de l'OCDE de 3.7 %).

Ces résultats quelque peu décevants devraient inciter les autorités danoises à étoffer encore les programmes des établissements d'enseignement primaire et secondaire du premier cycle. De vastes réformes sont en cours dans ces deux types d'établissements dans le but d'améliorer le niveau des résultats en compréhension de l'écrit, en sciences et en mathématiques.

Le gouvernement a créé en 2006 une nouvelle agence nationale chargée de l'assurance et de l'évaluation de la qualité dans les écoles primaires et les établissements d'enseignement secondaire du premier cycle. La même année, le Parlement danois a décidé de faire des évaluations nationales un outil pédagogique obligatoire dans ces écoles et ces établissements. Le principal objectif de la réforme nationale du système d'évaluation danois est de doter les enseignants d'un outil pédagogique susceptible de les aider à analyser le niveau de compétence de leurs élèves ainsi que le niveau de la classe. Cette démarche va dans le bon sens. La normalisation des évaluations crée un environnement dans lequel les écoles, les enseignants et les communes sont plus attentifs aux déterminants des résultats scolaires obtenus par les élèves.

Mais le Danemark a renoncé *a priori* à toute forme de classement des écoles fondé sur les notes obtenues lors des évaluations. Un certain nombre de raisons justifient le fait que l'on évite de diffuser les notes brutes individuelles. En particulier, les écarts de notation brute traduisent en général non seulement une diversité dans la qualité de l'enseignement mais aussi des différences dans les facteurs liés au milieu socioéconomique qui peuvent influencer les résultats des élèves. Toutefois, le caractère très restrictif de la stratégie danoise de diffusion des résultats diminue peut-être les incitations à l'amélioration car on ne fait guère de publicité autour de la médiocrité des résultats. En outre, le dispositif ne comporte aucun élément de responsabilisation de l'école car la médiocrité de ses performances n'engendre aucune conséquence. Il reste à voir si la politique danoise de « l'évaluation non sélective » (*soft testing*) constituera un moyen efficace d'apporter les changements attendus dans les performances des écoles.

---

12.   Enseignements primaire, secondaire et post-secondaire non tertiaire.

Un taux global de décrochage scolaire plus élevé que prévu

Le Danemark se caractérise aussi par un taux de décrochage scolaire relativement élevé. Ce taux était de 15.6 % parmi les jeunes âgés de 20 à 24 ans en 2008, et donc légèrement inférieur à la moyenne OCDE (16 %), mais bien supérieur aux taux correspondants observés dans les pays d'Europe centrale ou dans les autres pays nordiques comme la Suède (9 %) ou la Finlande (9.7 %). Conscientes de cette piètre performance de leur système éducatif, les autorités danoises se sont aujourd'hui engagées à ce que 95 % de chaque cohorte de jeunes obtienne un diplôme de l'enseignement secondaire supérieur d'ici 2015. Mais atteindre cet objectif ne sera pas chose facile à partir du taux de 83 % obtenu en 2007.

Le taux de décrochage scolaire relativement élevé du Danemark semble s'expliquer en partie par l'incapacité relative du système éducatif de base à inculquer les savoirs fondamentaux aux jeunes défavorisés. Les enquêtes PISA ont notamment démontré qu'au Danemark les enfants d'immigrés obtenaient de faibles résultats lors des évaluations et il existe des liens étroits entre la faiblesse des résultats dans les tests PISA et un niveau élevé de décrochage scolaire.

Un bon système d'éducation et formation professionnelles pour ceux qui vont jusqu'au bout

En revanche, le Danemark possède un bon système d'éducation et formation professionnelles pour les jeunes de 16 ans et plus. Ce système est relativement exigeant. Il faut en moyenne quatre ans pour obtenir un diplôme à l'issue d'un tel cursus. Selon des travaux de recherche, un bon niveau en mathématiques est le meilleur passeport pour réussir dans certaines filières professionnelles. Le système danois présente une forte dimension « d'alternance », synonyme : *i)* de mobilisation systématique des entreprises et des partenaires sociaux ; et *ii)* (partiellement de ce fait) d'une employabilité élevée des jeunes qui mènent à bien leurs études sous cette forme.

Toutefois, l'accès à ce système éducatif intervient tardivement, généralement après la fin de la scolarité obligatoire (16 ans) et après les années de césure que les jeunes Danois s'accordent traditionnellement avant d'entamer le deuxième cycle du secondaire. C'est cette seconde raison qui explique qu'en 2005, l'âge moyen de tous les élèves entreprenant une formation en alternance était pratiquement de 21 ans.

Le taux d'abandon est élevé, surtout parmi les jeunes immigrés qui ne sont pas originaires d'un pays occidental. L'entrée dans le « cours de base », la partie scolaire de la formation, est automatique pour tous les jeunes qui ont accompli neuf années d'enseignement élémentaire. L'accès à la formation pratique après le cours de base (partie appelée « cours principal ») est plus difficile car l'apprenti doit avoir trouvé préalablement un contrat d'apprentissage dans une entreprise. Les élèves doivent de fait se « débrouiller » presque tout seuls pour trouver une entreprise acceptant de les prendre comme apprenti. Quand ils ne trouvent pas de contrat d'apprentissage dans un domaine professionnel précis, beaucoup d'entre eux arrivent à en trouver un dans un autre domaine professionnel ou continuent dans un programme général du cycle secondaire supérieur. Cependant, on estime que 40 % de ceux qui décrochent à un moment de l'enseignement professionnel ne poursuivent aucune formation.

Les salaires des apprentis sont soumis à un régime spécial. Dans chaque secteur, un salaire minimum pour les apprentis est négocié tous les trois ans dans les conventions collectives de travail. L'apprenti, comme dans tout contrat de travail de droit commun, peut en outre négocier l'obtention d'un salaire plus élevé. Les entreprises reçoivent d'importantes subventions pour recruter et former les apprentis. Par conséquent, le coût moyen d'un apprenti ne représente que la moitié du coût d'un salarié de droit commun. Le salaire perçu par l'apprenti est cependant attractif pour un jeune car il est en moyenne 60 % plus élevé que l'allocation publique d'éducation.

Faire baisser le taux de décrochage dans ce type de formation tout en préservant la qualité des études

Inquiets à juste titre de l'incidence globale du décrochage des étudiants des formations professionnelles, les responsables de l'action publique s'efforcent d'améliorer la qualité du système de formation professionnelle (par des plans d'action que les établissements doivent obligatoirement mettre en place ou par le parrainage, par exemple). Ils ont aussi réformé ce type de formation pour tenir compte des besoins des individus situés en bas de l'échelle des compétences (programmes plus courts aboutissant à un diplôme partiel ou moins de travail en milieu scolaire, autrement dit moins de semaines à passer à l'école avant de commencer l'apprentissage dans une entreprise). L'enjeu n'en est pas moins d'améliorer les taux d'assiduité et de réussite sans compromettre la qualité, en particulier les bonnes dispositions des entreprises au regard du recrutement, de la formation et de la rémunération des apprentis.

Probablement les étudiants les plus âgés de l'OCDE

Au Danemark, la population d'étudiants et de diplômés compte probablement parmi les plus âgées des pays de l'OCDE. En d'autres termes, sauf à prendre effectivement leur retraite tardivement[13], les Danois passent moins d'années en emploi. D'aucuns font valoir que les étudiants « âgés » du Danemark ont accumulé une importante expérience du marché du travail car beaucoup ont exercé un emploi d'étudiant, ce qui leur a permis d'accéder à un emploi stable de manière plus rapide et plus facile. En effet, en 2008, environ 70 % des étudiants âgés de 23 à 24ans exerçaient un emploi. Il est vrai qu'en Australie, par exemple, les étudiants sont encore plus nombreux à travailler au même âge (78 %), mais il est vrai aussi qu'ils sont en moyenne beaucoup plus jeunes quand ils obtiennent leur diplôme.

Le retard dans l'achèvement des études commence à la fin de la scolarité obligatoire. Les étudiants s'engagent ainsi très fréquemment volontairement dans le dixième niveau[14] du cycle secondaire, même s'ils disposent des capacités scolaires pour poursuivre leur formation supérieure. On observe dès lors de longs temps de latence entre les deux cycles de l'enseignement secondaire. Un phénomène analogue est observé en fin d'études secondaires, au tournant des études supérieures. De surcroît, il n'est pas rare que les étudiants danois changent d'orientation pendant leurs études supérieures, ce qui implique qu'ils sont déjà avancés en âge quand ils entreprennent le cursus aboutissant au diplôme qu'ils finiront par obtenir.

Il est difficile de s'attaquer à ce problème car il n'existe pas de solution simple face à un phénomène profondément ancré dans la culture danoise. Parmi les éléments de réponse, on peut citer : i) une meilleure maîtrise des savoirs fondamentaux en fin de scolarité obligatoire pour améliorer le degré de « maturité pour l'apprentissage » des adolescents ; ii) une meilleure orientation scolaire ; et iii) une palette bien conçue de mesures d'incitation financière récompensant la précocité dans le commencement et l'achèvement des études supérieures.

---

13. Le taux d'emploi des 55-64 ans en 2008 au Danemark est effectivement plus élevé que dans l'OCDE ou l'Union européenne (respectivement 58 %, 54 % et 47 %).

14. Le dixième niveau a été conçu pour permettre aux étudiants en difficulté de rattraper les matières non suffisamment acquises pendant les neuf années de scolarité obligatoire et de clarifier leurs choix d'études secondaires supérieures.

Dans l'Accord de 2006 sur la protection sociale, un certain nombre de mesures étaient annoncées pour lutter contre le syndrome de l'achèvement tardif des études. En soi, la modification la plus importante consistait à faciliter l'accès à l'enseignement supérieur si l'élève n'attendait pas plus de deux ans après la fin de ses études secondaires pour s'inscrire. Dans le nouveau régime, les candidats aux études supérieures ont leur moyenne relevée de 1.08 et ont donc plus facilement accès à des cursus soumis à un *numerus clausus*. Toutefois, il y a fort à parier que cette mesure n'influera pas de manière significative sur le comportement des étudiants car l'accès libre est la règle pour la plupart des cursus.

Des mesures visant à faire changer les prestataires (c'est-à-dire les établissements d'enseignement supérieur) de mentalité ont également été annoncées dans l'Accord sur la protection sociale. En particulier, une nouvelle structure de financement devrait mieux harmoniser la durée effective des études avec la durée prévue. L'intention était aussi qu'une partie des subventions publiques soient payées aux prestataires uniquement lorsque les étudiants terminent leurs examens. Le rapport final de la Commission sur le marché du travail de 2007[15] propose également une série de mesures pour encourager un achèvement plus précoce des études.

Tout cela va dans le bon sens, mais d'autres décisions pourraient se révéler contreproductives. Par exemple, la décision d'augmenter le plafond de rémunération des étudiants leur permet de gagner plus tout en continuant à percevoir le montant intégral de leur allocation d'études et risque en réalité de retarder l'achèvement des études. Des chercheurs ont montré que plus les revenus propres de l'étudiant sont élevés, plus celui-ci prend du temps pour terminer ses études. On remarquera à cet égard qu'en Suède, le Conseil de la politique budgétaire a recommandé d'abaisser les niveaux de rémunération de manière à encourager les étudiants à travailler moins et à se concentrer sur leurs études.

Pour s'assurer que tous les jeunes acquièrent les savoirs fondamentaux nécessaires à l'entrée dans la vie active et à la progression professionnelle, et pour les inciter à mettre rapidement ces savoirs en application, les mesures suivantes pourraient être envisagées :

---

15. La Commission sur le marché du travail a été établie en 2007 pour faire des recommandations sur la façon d'atteindre les objectifs d'emploi requis par le Plan 2015 de politique budgétaire du gouvernement. Elle a remis son rapport final en août 2009.

- *Faire progresser la réforme nationale des évaluations dans l'enseignement primaire et le premier cycle du secondaire et veiller à ce que les écoles soient davantage tenues de rendre des comptes.* Des éléments d'observation internationale montrent que les normes définies de l'extérieur telles que celles exposées dans la réforme nationale des évaluations adoptée en 2006 aident à lutter contre la tendance des enseignants à revoir à la baisse leurs attentes et leurs exigences quand ils sont face à des élèves vraisemblablement moins doués. S'il y a de bonnes raisons de prévenir la diffusion des notes brutes individuelles, la décision du Danemark de ne pas divulguer les classements des écoles fondés sur les notes obtenues lors des évaluations devrait être reconsidérée. Il conviendrait en outre de réfléchir à des éléments sur lesquels les écoles devraient rendre des comptes, qui seraient basés sur des résultats vérifiables (progrès des élèves dans les matières fondamentales, par exemple).

- *S'attaquer au taux de décrochage élevé dans les programmes d'éducation et formation professionnelles.* Les jeunes devraient être mieux préparés avant d'entamer le cours de base d'un programme d'éducation et formation professionnelles. Il faudrait leur offrir plus de possibilités de formations pratiques grâce aux « production schools »[16] ainsi qu'un meilleur suivi individuel dans les systèmes primaire et secondaire inférieur. Les centres d'orientation pour les jeunes devraient mieux aider les jeunes quand ils s'inscrivent au cours principal et cherchent une place d'apprentissage dans une entreprise. Il est important que le SPE et les centres d'orientation pour les jeunes coopèrent étroitement pour recueillir plus de places d'apprentissage.

- *Investir dans une véritable stratégie d'« activation » visant à réduire le délai global d'obtention du diplôme.* La lourdeur de la fiscalité et la générosité des allocations d'études ont, quand elles se conjuguent, des effets pervers car elles incitent les jeunes à prendre de longues pauses entre la fin de leurs études secondaires et le début de leurs études supérieures, et à faire durer leurs études une fois qu'ils les ont commencées. Si modifier la combinaison actuelle fiscalité directe élevée/allocations d'études généreuses

---

16. Depuis 1978, ces écoles offrent aux jeunes de 16 ans et plus qui ne sont pas prêts pour suivre un programme normal d'éducation et formation professionnelles l'opportunité de participer à une formation pratique dans différents domaines qui vont de la métallurgie, la charpente et le textile aux media, au théâtre et à la musique.

semble difficile à envisager, il convient que le Danemark élabore une stratégie d'activation[17] ambitieuse ciblant les étudiants mais aussi les établissements. Cette stratégie aurait pour objectif explicite d'inciter les établissements à pousser les étudiants à commencer et à terminer leurs études dans les temps, et d'inciter les étudiants à adopter ce comportement. Un des moyens pourrait être d'ajuster les allocations d'études en faveur de débuts précoces et de poursuite dans les délais prévus. En même temps, les dispositifs « taximètres » à taux plein[18] finançant les établissements d'enseignement supérieur ne devraient exister que pour ceux qui recrutent des étudiants n'ayant pas différé leur cursus et le menant rapidement jusqu'à son terme.

S'attaquer aux barrières qui existent du côté de la demande pour promouvoir de meilleurs emplois pour plus de jeunes

Jusqu'au milieu de l'année 2008, le Danemark se caractérisait par l'extrême tension de son marché du travail. L'utilisation des capacités augmentait, son niveau approchant des records historiques, et l'obstacle que constituait l'aggravation des pénuries de main-d'œuvre qualifiée est devenu une contrainte plus proéminente. Mais un marché tendu implique également de meilleures perspectives d'emploi pour les travailleurs peu qualifiés ou immigrés.

Enjeux de politique à court terme créés par la récession

Le ralentissement économique actuel remet en question certains des très bons résultats du Danemark au regard du marché du travail. Face à un tassement rapide de l'activité, la première réaction des entreprises est de cesser de recruter avant d'entamer le processus plus coûteux des licenciements. Comme les jeunes sont évidemment nettement surreprésentés parmi ceux qui recherchent un emploi, ils sont aussi les plus touchés en cas de gel des recrutements.

En outre, il est moins coûteux pour une entreprise de licencier des jeunes que des travailleurs appartenant à des classes d'âge de forte activité. Parce que les jeunes sont moins expérimentés, leur licenciement implique, pour leur entreprise, une plus faible perte de savoir-faire spécifique. De surcroît, les jeunes travailleurs ont moins

---

17.   Reprenant les principes qui ont été mis en œuvre avec succès dans le cas des prestations sociales.

18.   Version danoise du système des chèques-éducation.

d'ancienneté dans l'emploi et occupent souvent des emplois temporaires. Ces deux facteurs réduisent les coûts de licenciement à la charge des employeurs. Souvent, les jeunes sont aussi les premiers à partir en période de retournement conjoncturel, ce qui illustre le phénomène du « dernier arrivé, premier parti ».

Il convient néanmoins de souligner qu'au Danemark, il n'y a pas de différence dans le niveau de protection de l'emploi prévu par la loi ou les réglementations, que l'on soit jeune travailleur ou travailleur plus âgé[19]. C'est une conséquence de la tradition danoise de la flexibilité du marché du travail, qui fait partie du modèle de flexicurité, qui veut qu'un salarié du secteur privé puisse être licencié facilement. Ceci implique que, toutes choses égales par ailleurs, le coût global de la crise économique en termes de destructions d'emplois devrait moins se concentrer sur les jeunes travailleurs au Danemark que dans d'autres pays de l'OCDE. Pour autant, il peut être judicieux de s'attacher à remédier au handicap dont les jeunes tendent à souffrir quand la demande de main-d'œuvre diminue. Rendre les jeunes à risque plus attrayants aux yeux des employeurs en abaissant les coûts du travail (à condition d'en faire une mesure temporaire à caractère sélectif) est une méthode permettant d'atteindre cet objectif.

Pour mieux faire face à la crise actuelle et lever les obstacles structurels à l'emploi des jeunes qui subsistent côté demande, il conviendrait de réfléchir aux mesures exposées ci-dessous :

- *Dans cette période de baisse de la demande de travail, les partenaires sociaux pourraient explorer diverses possibilités de réduire temporairement le coût du travail des jeunes peu qualifiés.* Concrètement, cela pourrait être réalisé en étendant à tous les jeunes ayant « décroché » de l'école (les moins de 25 ans, par exemple) le régime salarial que les secteurs d'activité/entreprises appliquent actuellement aux apprentis de l'enseignement professionnel. Cela permettrait d'augmenter le degré de différenciation des revenus entre les différents niveaux d'instruction ainsi que les incitations à investir dans le capital humain : il s'agit là d'une mesure qui devrait *a priori* contribuer à réduire l'incidence du décrochage scolaire. Une telle mesure devrait faire l'objet d'une évaluation peu de temps après sa mise en œuvre de manière à décider si elle doit être abolie dès le début de la reprise.

---

19.   Contrairement à ce qui se passe en Espagne, en France ou en Pologne, par exemple.

- *Alternativement, le même effet sur la demande de travailleurs jeunes peut être atteint à travers des subventions salariales plus généreuses dans le secteur privé pour les jeunes défavorisés.* Le gouvernement danois vient d'annoncer de telles subventions pour les jeunes qui perçoivent des allocations sociales depuis plus d'un an. Une telle mesure devrait être évaluée après un certain temps pour s'assurer qu'elle est efficace en termes de coût et décider de son maintien à plus long terme.

Renforcer l'activation pour mieux aider les jeunes défavorisés

Prestations généreuses assorties de mesures d'activation

Au Danemark, les jeunes chômeurs sont couverts par un des systèmes de garantie de revenu les plus généreux de la zone OCDE. Le taux de compensation net représenté par les prestations d'assurance chômage compte parmi les plus élevés de l'OCDE, et la durée maximum de versement de ces prestations (quatre ans) est également l'une des plus longues. L'aide sociale soumise à des critères de ressources[20] est elle aussi généreuse d'après les comparaisons internationales : peuvent en bénéficier toutes les personnes âgées de 18 ans ou plus qui n'ont pas (ou plus) droit aux indemnités d'assurance chômage.

S'il est vrai que les dispositifs d'aide sociale relativement généreux risquent *a priori* de constituer des pièges du chômage, au Danemark les mesures d'activation ciblées sur les jeunes favorisent le retour rapide à l'emploi et donnent des résultats concluants. Comme nous l'avons déjà dit, c'est le résultat d'une application rigoureuse et bien pensée d'une activation selon le principe des « obligations réciproques » introduit au milieu des années 90 en vertu duquel, en contrepartie de la garantie de revenu, les demandeurs d'emploi (y compris les jeunes) doivent participer à des activités de formation, de recherche d'emploi ou de placement dans un travail (l'approche flexicurité). Un refus de participer peut entraîner une sanction portant sur l'allocation.

Au cours de la deuxième moitié des années 90 et au début des années 2000, l'activation a été affinée et renforcée, surtout à l'égard des jeunes, apparemment avec succès. Avant le ralentissement économique actuel, le chômage de longue durée des jeunes était extrêmement faible au Danemark par rapport aux autres pays. En 2008, il représentait 6.4 %

---

20.   Au Danemark, l'octroi de l'aide sociale est subordonné à des critères de ressources prenant en compte le revenu et le patrimoine de la famille.

du chômage total des jeunes Danois, contre 23.9 % dans l'Union européenne et 18.8 % dans la zone OCDE.

Depuis août 2009, le SPE a été décentralisé plus avant et la mise en œuvre des programmes actifs du marché du travail est de la responsabilité des communes. La distinction qui prévalait auparavant entre les bureaux nationaux qui géraient les allocations des assurés contre le chômage et les bureaux locaux qui géraient celles des bénéficiaires d'allocations sociales n'existe plus. Tous les demandeurs d'emploi vont dorénavant être pris en charge par la même agence (guichet unique) dans chaque commune. Cependant, cette nouvelle organisation comporte un risque de diversité accrue dans les services offerts d'une commune à l'autre, même si des dispositions ont été prises pour vérifier leur cohérence avec les mesures d'emploi au niveau national. Il est important que ce processus de décentralisation soit soigneusement évalué dès le début pour s'assurer que des services efficaces sont mis en place, en particulier pour les jeunes.

Intervention rapide et activation pendant six mois pour tous les allocataires de moins de 30 ans

A partir de l'été 2009, après un premier entretien individuel au cours du premier (auparavant troisième) mois de chômage et un maximum de trois (auparavant six mois), tous les Danois de moins de 30 ans qui perçoivent une allocation d'assurance chômage ou d'aide sociale doivent prendre part à un programme d'activation. Cependant, les règles d'activation sont plus strictes pour les jeunes de moins de 25 ans qui n'ont pas de diplôme du secondaire supérieur et qui n'ont pas d'enfants. Ces derniers sont obligés d'intégrer un programme éducatif, soit dans le système d'enseignement ordinaire s'ils sont capables de le faire, soit dans le cas contraire dans un programme spécial d'éducation qui les remette à niveau pour intégrer le système d'enseignement ordinaire. Par contre, toute mesure d'activation peut être offerte aux jeunes de 25 à 29 ans et aux jeunes qui ont des enfants.

De plus, depuis 1996 et l'adoption du Programme de lutte contre le chômage des jeunes, les individus âgés de 18 à 24 ans n'ayant pas de diplôme équivalent au secondaire supérieur ont leurs indemnités d'assurance chômage réduites de 50 % (proche du niveau de l'allocation d'éducation) au bout de six mois de chômage, et sont tenus d'intégrer un programme spécial d'éducation. La réduction des allocations après six mois d'activation a été progressivement étendue à tous les jeunes de moins de 25 ans qui reçoivent une allocation sociale. Par contre, pour les bénéficiaires de 25-29 ans et tous les jeunes qui ont des enfants, l'allocation n'est pas réduite, même s'ils ont un faible niveau de qualification. Il apparaît pourtant que ces groupes tendent à bénéficier plus longtemps d'allocations sociales, également parce qu'ils ont des incitations plus faibles à (re)trouver rapidement un emploi.

Effet « menace » ou effet « programme » ?

Si l'on remonte aux années 80, on constate que les deux composantes de ce qu'il est convenu d'appeler le modèle de « flexicurité » (souplesse de la réglementation de l'emploi et générosité des prestations d'aide sociale) faisaient déjà partie du paysage danois de l'emploi, mais les taux de chômage étaient relativement élevés. Leur impact potentiel sur la durée du chômage a été sensiblement renforcé par l'application plus rigoureuse des critères d'admissibilité à la recherche d'emploi et par des stratégies renforcées de retour à l'emploi, deux importants éléments de ce qu'il est convenu d'appeler la « stratégie d'activation ».

Mais les politiques d'activation sont coûteuses. Compte tenu de l'utilisation très large qui est faite de ces politiques au Danemark, il n'est pas étonnant que les dépenses publiques affectées aux programmes actifs du marché du travail[21] (1 % du PIB en 2007) soient beaucoup plus élevées que la moyenne de l'OCDE (0.4 % du PIB) et parmi les plus élevées de celles observées dans les pays de l'OCDE. Selon différentes études, les politiques d'activation ont un puissant effet de menace alors que d'après les données d'observation, les effets des programmes actifs sont contrastés.

Préconiser l'emploi ou le retour vers l'éducation ?

Dans le passé, de nombreux programmes actifs du marché du travail des pays de l'OCDE ont été élaborés suivant le principe du « travail contre allocation ». Mais au cours de l'actuel ralentissement conjoncturel, la réorientation de la stratégie abandonnant le principe du « travail d'abord » au profit des « compétences d'abord », qui privilégie l'éducation et la formation et non le placement immédiat dans un emploi, s'observe dans un certain nombre de pays de l'OCDE en faveur des jeunes défavorisés. Au Danemark, le Programme de lutte contre le chômage des jeunes, par exemple, a déjà manifestement eu un effet positif sur le taux de transition vers l'éducation alors que l'effet sur le passage immédiat à l'emploi n'est pas aussi certain. Selon des études internationales, une stratégie d'activation privilégiant le travail donne

---

21. Hors SPE et administration.

de meilleurs résultats pour les jeunes qualifiés qui sont prêts à occuper un emploi, mais une stratégie privilégiant l'acquisition de compétences convient mieux aux jeunes défavorisés qui, souvent, ne possèdent pas les qualifications dont le marché du travail a besoin. Au cours du ralentissement économique actuel, une réorientation vers une stratégie privilégiant l'acquisition de compétences pourrait aider les jeunes peu qualifiés à être mieux armés pour la reprise.

Pour améliorer l'efficacité du système d'action sociale danois à l'égard des jeunes, les mesures suivantes pourraient être envisagées :

- *Mettre en place des incitations financières plus fortes à sortir du système des allocations sociales pour les jeunes de 25 à 29 ans possédant un faible niveau d'éducation.* Certains analystes danois et la Commission du marché du travail ont recommandé l'extension des règles plus strictes régissant l'octroi des prestations sociales aux jeunes jusqu'à l'âge de 30 ans. Cette réforme pourrait être mise en œuvre promptement. Cependant, les jeunes parents ne devraient pas être *a priori* considérés comme un groupe à exempter de la stratégie normale d'activation.

- *S'assurer que les activités de remise à niveau des compétences sont bien adaptées au profil des jeunes sans emploi et en particulier, à ceux qui ont décroché de l'école.* Il faut donner aujourd'hui de plus en plus de place aux activités de remise à niveau des compétences. L'orientation vers une stratégie privilégiant les compétences devrait être envisagée pour les jeunes les plus défavorisés. Il importe d'éviter la solution du « retour à l'école » pour les jeunes qui ont décroché car elle risque de se révéler extrêmement contreproductive. Il semblerait, d'après les évaluations danoises, que seuls les programmes de formation comportant un fort élément « d'apprentissage sur le tas » aient un impact positif sur les perspectives d'emploi et de salaires d'après-programme. Il faut donc continuer d'accorder la priorité aux programmes dont l'enseignement est dispensé hors des établissements scolaires traditionnels, et mettre les jeunes régulièrement en contact avec le milieu du travail pour qu'ils acquièrent une expérience professionnelle, de préférence sous l'égide d'organisations impliquées de longue date dans le placement en emploi ou le conseil.

- *Développer une dimension « résidentielle » dans l'arsenal de mesures visant les jeunes très défavorisés.* Il y a peu de chances que les programmes actifs du marché du travail standards fonctionnent pour les jeunes les plus défavorisés qui cumulent habituellement les facteurs de risque sociaux (faible niveau d'instruction, appartenance à une minorité ethnique, toxicomanie, maladie mentale, etc.). Pour cette population, des solutions plus radicales et plus coûteuses sont probablement nécessaires. Une possibilité (s'appuyant sur les écoles de production et les *Folk High Schools*[22] comme points de départ) serait de proposer systématiquement un cadre scolaire du type internat offrant à la fois : *i)* un accompagnement par des adultes ; *ii)* la mise en situation de travail/acquisition d'expérience ; et *iii)* des cours de rattrapage. Pour cette initiative, il serait possible de s'inspirer, par exemple, du programme *Job Corps* qui existe depuis longtemps aux États-Unis.

22.　　Des programmes résidentiels d'éducation centrés sur les valeurs existentielles traditionnelles danoises mais qui n'offrent pas de diplôme reconnu.

INTRODUCTION

Improving the performance of youth in the labour market is a crucial challenge in OECD countries. Declines in the number of new entrants to the labour market and ageing populations and workforces do not seem to have translated into much better labour market outcomes for youth. Thus it remains crucial to maintain or reinforce policies aimed at better equipping young people with the skills required by the labour market and helping them accomplish a successful transition from school to work.

The Danish government is particularly concerned about how well prepared young people are for the labour market. It is also aware of the need to develop labour market and welfare institutions that are likely to maximise youth opportunities. While Danish youth face a lower risk of unemployment than in many other OECD countries, the future economic outlook resulting from the global economic crisis is uncertain. Several barriers to youth employment persist.

On the (labour) supply side, some young people still lack the basic skills they need to succeed in a career. More generally, the proportion of young Danes entering the labour market with at least an upper secondary qualification is still lower than in most OECD countries. This could partially explain the intensity of the skill shortages the country was facing before the recent economic slowdown. Other barriers exist too. Students for instance probably also lack incentives to graduate quickly.

The purpose of this report is to examine all these barriers and discuss how education, training, labour market and social policies may help improve the school-to-work transition. Chapter 1 presents basic facts on the situation of youth in the Danish labour market. The role of education and training in shaping the transition from school to the labour market is analysed in Chapter 2. Demand-side barriers and opportunities to youth employment in the current downturn are explored in Chapter 3. Finally, Chapter 4 analyses the role of welfare benefits and the Public Employment Service in helping non-employed youth to get a job.

CHAPTER 1

THE CHALLENGE AHEAD

Until very recently, the Danish economy was reaping the benefits of a long uninterrupted spell of growth that contributed to the emergence of tight labour markets. The country's good macro-economic performance over the past decade translated into many job opportunities. As a result, the standardised unemployment rate declined to 3.2% in early 2008, the lowest rate recorded since the early 1980s.

These trends have contributed to an improvement in the youth labour market performance, which was already good by international standards. However, good macro-economic and labour market performances were insufficient to solve the problems faced on the labour market by some groups of youth, particularly school drop-outs and the children of immigrants of non-European origin.

The purpose of this chapter is to examine how the Danish youth labour market performance compared with other OECD countries before the start of the crisis, in general as well as for various categories of youth. The chapter draws a picture of demographics and the position of Danish youth in the labour market (Section 1) and then examines the school-to-work transition and the type (part-time/full-time, temporary/permanent) of jobs held by youth (Section 2).

1. Demographics and main labour market outcomes

A. The share of young people (15-24) in the working-age population has declined since the 1970s

Figure 1.1 shows that the share of young people in the working-age population has declined in almost all OECD countries since 1975. The OECD average was 27% in the second half of the 1970s and is now just above 20%. There is, of course, some cross-country variation: the downward trend has been more pronounced in Korea than in Mexico, for instance.

Nevertheless, it is visible across most countries. Historically, Denmark has been well below the OECD average according to the relative size of younger cohorts. However, this indicator is projected to increase between 2005 and 2025 showing the country in a position that is close to the OECD average. This upward trend is partly due to immigration flows which have increased significantly since the mid-1980s. There has been a gradual shift in the composition of immigration with a strong increase in labour migration and stabilising levels of humanitarian migration and family reunification (see Box 1.1).

Figure 1.1. **Decreasing share of youth in the working-age population, OECD countries, 1975-2025**[a]

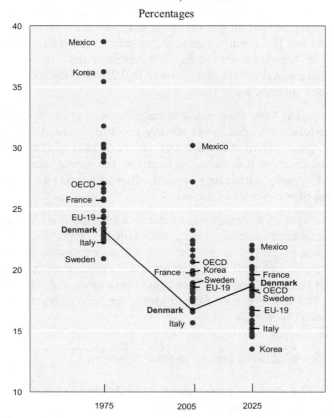

a) Ratio of the population aged 15 to 24 to the population aged 15 to 64.

Source: National projections: 2007 for Australia, Austria, Canada, the Czech Republic, Denmark, Finland, France, Greece, Iceland, Japan, Korea, the Netherlands, New Zealand, Norway, Portugal, the Slovak Republic, Sweden, Switzerland and the United States; 2006 for Belgium, Hungary, Italy, Turkey; and the United Kingdom; 2005 for Mexico. Eurostat projections: 2007 for Ireland, Poland and Spain; 2006 for Germany and Luxembourg.

Box 1.1. Immigration in Denmark in recent years

Traditionally, Denmark has not regarded itself as a country of immigration. This is due to its relatively homogeneous population of 5.4 million, a strong sense of national identity, and the fact that, until recently, immigration flows were moderate. Prior to the 1980s, immigration to Denmark was a very marginal phenomenon (Liebig, 2007). Despite the rapid growth since then, with less than 7% immigrants in the population, Denmark still has one of the smallest immigrant populations in western Europe.

Immigration to Denmark in the past has been strongly dominated by refugees and family reunification – groups whose labour market outcomes tend to be not as good as the native-born or economic migrants, particularly in the early years of settlement.

More recently, specific labour shortages have led Denmark to focus on recruitment of qualified workers from abroad and Poland became mid-2000s the major country of origin of immigrants. Labour migration continues to rise in 2007: most residence permits were issued for employment, followed by education and family reunification.

Source: Liebig (2007), OECD (2007) and OECD (2009d).

B.   *Low levels of youth unemployment*

Judged in terms of unemployment, the Danish youth labour market performance is good in international comparison. The youth (15-24) unemployment rate reached 7.2% in 2008, 6 percentage points below the OECD average (Figure 1.2, Panel B), and the lowest level recorded since the early 1980s. These positive results should be at least partially attributed to the robust economic growth that prevailed until recently.

On the positive side, it also is important to stress that the incidence of long-term unemployment[23] – the most problematic form of unemployment – is low amongst youth in Denmark (Figure 1.3): 6.4% of total youth unemployment in 2008 *versus* an OECD average of 18.8%. Finally, youth employment rates were high, at 68.5 % in 2008, 25 percentage points above the OECD average (Figure 1.2, Panel A).

---

23.   Unemployment spells lasting more than one year.

Figure 1.2.   **Youth[a] unemployment and employment indicators, Denmark, OECD and Europe, 1983-2008**

Percentages and ratios

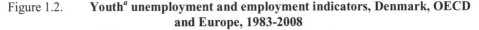

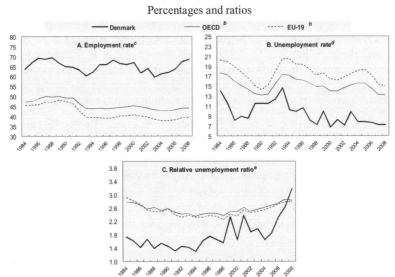

a)   Youth aged 16-24 for Iceland, Norway (until 2006), Spain, Sweden, the United Kingdom and the United States; youth aged 15-24 for all other countries.
b)   Unweighted averages.
c)   Employed as a percentage of the population in the age group.
d)   Unemployed as a percentage of the labour force in the age group.
e)   Unemployment rate of youth (15/16-24)/unemployment rate of adults (25-54).

Source: National labour force surveys.

Figure 1.3.   **Incidence of long-term[a] unemployment among youth,[b] OECD countries,[c] 1998 and 2008**

Percentages of unemployed youth

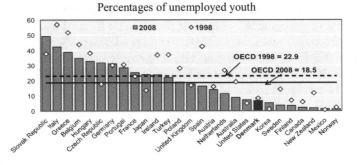

a)   12 months and over.
b)   Youth aged 16-24 for Norway (for 1998 only), Spain, Sweden, the United Kingdom and the United States; youth aged 15-24 for all other countries.
c)   Unweighted average of countries shown.

Source: National labour force surveys.

C.   Distribution of risk of unemployment

If in 2007 in Denmark, the children of immigrants did not experience a high unemployment rate by international standards (around 6%); they had poorer labour outcomes than the children of natives (see Box 1.2). Their relative risk of being unemployed appears in particular above the average for other European countries. They form nevertheless only a small group in Denmark, (in 2007, only about 2% of the 20-29 are native-born children of immigrants), but their number is growing rapidly.

The risk of unemployment is high also in Denmark for young adults aged 20-29 who have less than an upper secondary qualification[24] (Figure 1.4). Their rate of unemployment at 8.8% was higher in 2008 than the 3.5% characterising young adults with at least an upper secondary education (ISCED 3 or more) (on the horizontal axis) and their relative risk of being unemployed (ratio on the vertical axis) is close to the European average. In 2008, the ratio was 2.5 times that of more educated young Danes, whereas it was of 2.7 for young Europeans on average.

Box 1.2. **Children of immigrants in Denmark have higher unemployment rates than the children of natives**

The OECD Secretariat has collected comparative data in 16 OECD countries on the situation of the native-born children of immigrants having left education (Liebig and Widmaier, 2009). On average over the OECD countries for which comparative data are available, the children of immigrants have an unemployment rate that is 1.7 (1.6) times higher than that of the children of natives for men (women) (see figure below). According to the same study, the children of immigrants also have lower employment rates. Part of the differences in labour market performance observed in most European countries is due to the fact that the children of immigrants tend to have a lower educational attainment than the children of natives. Liebig and Widmaier (2009) stress, however, that significant gaps remain in many countries, including Denmark, even after correcting for differences in average educational attainment.

In Denmark, the children of immigrants are not experiencing a dramatic absolute level of unemployment. For both men and women, the unemployment rate is near 6%, one of the lowest among OECD countries. However, their relative performance compared with the one of the children of natives is particularly poor for native-born boys of immigrants.

---

24.   This corresponds to the level 3 of the International Standard Classification of Education (ISCED 3).

Unemployment rates[a] of youth aged 20-29 having left education, by immigrant status[b] and gender, around 2007 in a selection of OECD countries[c]

As a percentage of the labour force in each category

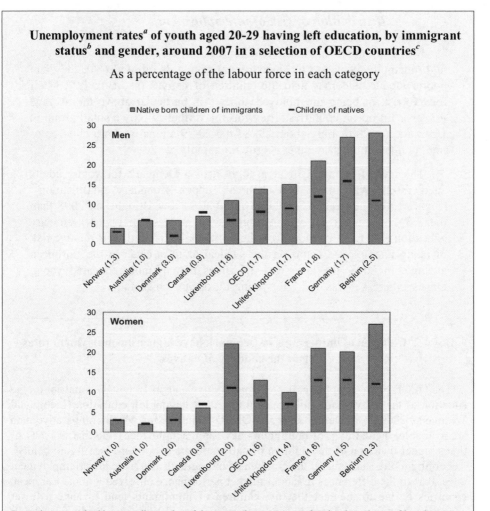

Countries are ranked in ascending order of the unemployment rate of native-born boys of immigrants.

a) Unemployment rate of native-born children of immigrants/unemployment rate of children of natives in parenthesis.

b) Children of natives are defined as children born in the country with at least one parent native-born. Native-born children of immigrants refer to children with both parents foreign-born.

c) Unweighted average of countries shown.

Source: Liebig and Widmaier (2009).

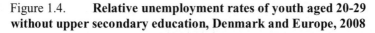

Figure 1.4.   **Relative unemployment rates of youth aged 20-29 without upper secondary education, Denmark and Europe, 2008**

Percentages and ratios[a]

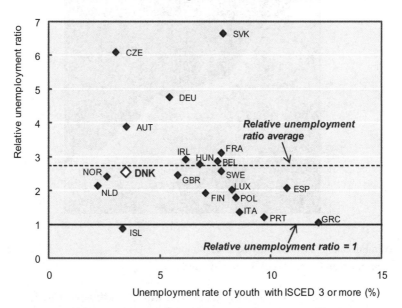

a)   The vertical axis displays the ratio between the unemployment rate of youth without ISCED 3 and that of youth with ISCED 3 or more.

Source: European Labour Force Survey (EULFS).

2. Transition from school to work

The transition from school to work involves more than just passing from an educational institution to the labour market. In Denmark, particularly, the school-to-work transition covers a broad period during which students combine study and work (Figure 1.5). They then leave education and start looking for more stable jobs.

Figure 1.5.   **Activity status of youth by single year of age, Denmark, 2008**

Percentages

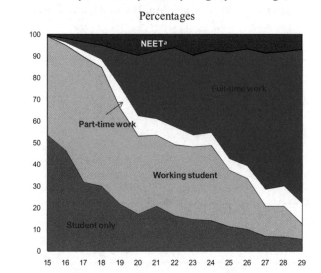

a)   Neither in Education nor in Employment or Training.

Source: European Union Labour Force Survey (EULFS).

Figure 1.6.   **Combining study and work, youth aged 16-24,
Denmark and selected OECD countries, 2008[a]**

Percentages of students by age group

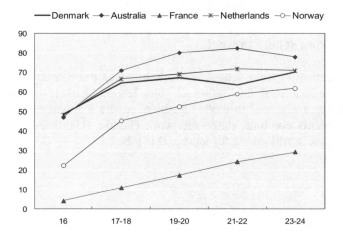

a)   2006 for Australia.

Source: European Union Labour Force Survey (EULFS) and Melbourne Institute, Household, Income and Labour Dynamics in Australia Survey (HILDA), Release 6 for Australia.

A.   *Young Danes enter the labour market when still students*

Most young Danes have their first contact with the labour market when they are still students. In 2008, up to 48% of those aged 16 held student jobs (Figure 1.6). For those aged 23-24, the share rose to 70%, which is just below the Dutch rate of 71% known to be one of the highest in Europe.

B.   *But students are remarkably old when they graduate*

More than 24% of young Danes declared in 2008 that they were still students while aged 25-29 (Figure 1.7, horizontal axis). This is, with Finland and Iceland, more than anywhere else in Europe. An interesting feature is that these high attendance rates have no apparent positive impact on more tertiary educational attainment among adults aged 30-34 (Figure 1.7, vertical axis). In particular, the larger share of Danish students aged 25-29 does not translate into achieving significantly more human capital. In 2008, in Denmark the share of adults aged 30-34 with a teriary level was 45% compared with 53.4% in Ireland where the share of "old" students was much lower (9.6%).

Figure 1.7.   **Share of students aged 25-29 and share of tertiary degrees**[a] **among adults (aged 30-34), Denmark and selected OECD countries, 2008**[b]

Percentages

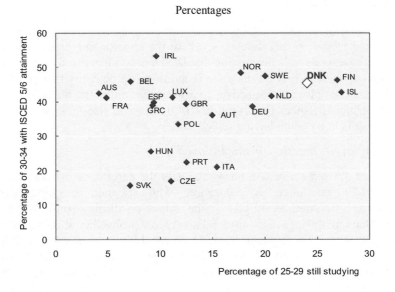

a)   ISCED 5/6 refers to tertiary education.
b)   2006 for Australia.

Source: European Union Labour Force Survey (EULFS), and Melbourne Institute, Household, Income and Labour Dynamics in Australia Survey (HILDA), Release 6 for Australia.

Some argue that older students in Denmark have accumulated significant labour market experience as many hold student jobs, which may help them have a faster transition to stable jobs. Mid-2000 a large majority of Danish students aged 21 and over had indeed such a job (Figure 1.6). Nevertheless, even more Australian students (80%) for instance work but still managed to graduate before turning 25. Many indicators in (OECD, 2009b) suggest that they also have a very rapid school-to-work transition. The tentative conclusion is that Denmark perhaps needs to "activate" its students whereas Australia does not face such a problem.

C.   *After leaving education*

Most of the labour market indicators presented so far are primarily age-based. Consequently, they amalgamate: *i)* individuals who are still in education; and *ii)* individuals who have left education and are potentially entirely available for the labour market. In a review on school-to-work transition, it appears reasonable to try to assess the labour market situation of those who have left education. This is not an easy task, due do the lack of adequate international data sets that comprise simultaneously young Danes and a reasonable number of other OECD countries.

No longer studying

One first option is to exploit labour-force-survey-like data to compute conditional labour market outcomes, where the conditioning aspect simply rests on the respondent's declaration that he/she is no longer studying. Using that option, one can first estimate the (conditional) probability that youth is employed, unemployed or inactive, following the traditional breakdown of the International Labour Organisation (ILO). One can also look at the type of contract held by youth having left education.

Non-employed: inactive or unemployed?

Figure 1.8 reports on the horizontal axis the percentage of individuals aged 20-29, no longer in education, who are not in employment (alternatively referred as NEET).[25] The values on display confirm that a young Dane (male or female) has a relatively low probability of being out of employment after leaving education. That probability was of 9.8% in 2008 for young men aged 20-29, below the European average of 14.5%. The corresponding figures for young women were 15.6% (Denmark) and 26.3% (European average).

---

25.   Neither in education, nor in employment or training, see also Figure 1.5.

Figure 1.8.   **Being non-employed after leaving school by gender,**
youth aged 20-29, Denmark and Europe,[a] 2008

Percentages

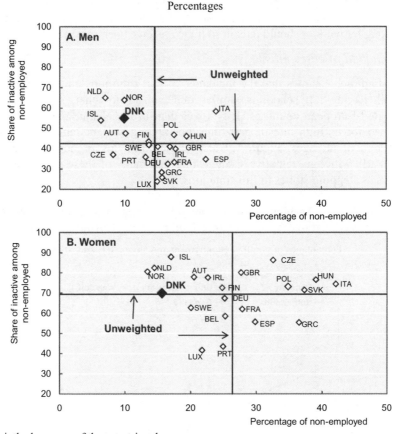

a)   Unweigthed average of the countries shown.
Source: European Union Labour Force Survey (EULFS).

Figure 1.8 also reveals on the vertical axis that being male and non-employed in Denmark generally means being "inactive" rather than unemployed. More than 55% of young men with no employment in Denmark in 2008 were inactive and thus outside the labour force. That share was only 43% on average across European countries. The propensity of non-employed Danish women to remain inactive was more in line with the European average, although at 70% it was intrinsically higher than that observed among men.

Having a larger or smaller share of inactive *versus* unemployed youth may not be of great importance, particularly if the total formed by the addition of two groups is not extremely large. However, one may argue that it is preferable that youth are unemployed rather that inactive. According to the ILO definition, unemployed people are more closely connected to the labour market than inactive ones: they are "available for the labour market" and are actively looking for work or should remain so if they receive unemployment benefits.

What kind of entry jobs?

Figure 1.9 shows that the incidence of part-time jobs among employed youth having left school is similar in Denmark to what is observed in selected European countries. It is lower than in the Netherlands, a country known for its high rate of part-time jobs among students and also among workers of all ages. Figure 1.9 also shows that this proportion declines regularly with age, tentatively suggesting that many of these part-time jobs serve as stepping stones to full-time jobs.

Figure 1.9.   **Incidence of part-time jobs among youth in employment[a]
no longer in education,[b] by age, Denmark and selected European countries, 2008**

Percentages of youth in employment and having left education

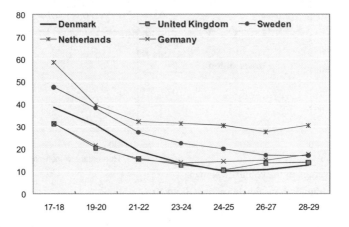

a)   Youth aged 17-29.
b)   Based on the respondent's declaration that he/she is no longer a student when asked about his/her main status.
Source: European Union Labour Force Survey (EULFS).

Figure 1.10 reports the share of youth in temporary contracts by age. It shows that in Denmark the prevalence of these contracts is well below that of many other European countries. The negative age gradient is also visible, and supportive of the stepping-stone assumption, at least at a very aggregate level.

Figure 1.10.   **Incidence of temporary jobs among youth in employment[a]**
no longer in education,[b] by age, Denmark and selected European countries, 2008

Percentages of youth in employment and having left education

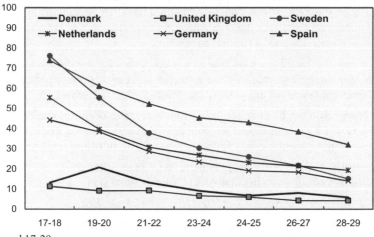

a)   Youth aged 17-29.
b)   Based on the respondent's declaration that he/she is no longer a student when asked about his/her main status.

Source: European Union Labour Force Survey (EULFS).

Expected years in employment following the end of education

Most labour force surveys, like the European Union Labour Force Survey (EULFS), ask respondents about the year they completed initial education. In the case of Denmark, this information can be obtained from every wave of the EULFS survey. It can be used to compute the expected number of years spent in employment during the five years after leaving education (Box 1.3 for the methodology).

This indicator (Figure 1.11) shows that a typical young Dane will have spent 4.5 years in employment during his/her five first years after leaving education, which is higher than the 4.4 years recorded in the other best OECD performers: the Netherlands, Australia and Switzerland. Moreover, the gap between highly educated (*i.e.* with more than ISCED 3) and school drop-outs (*i.e.* with less than ISCED 3) is lower, at 0.5 year, than among most of the other countries examined. There is thus in Denmark less diversity of outcomes between highly-educated and low-educated youth in terms of the expected number of years in employment during the five years after the completion of education.

Box 1.3. **Computing the expected number of years spent in employment during the five years after leaving school**

Labour force surveys are not longitudinal data sets. However, they generally contain information on the year of completion of highest level of education. In combination with information on the age of the respondent, this item can be used to compute a proxy of the duration since the end of (initial) education.

Then, using the distribution of labour market status by duration since the end of education, it is possible to calculate the expected number of years a typical respondent has spent in employment (or any other status) since he/she left school.

This computation can be done for the various categories (k) of respondents: *e.g.* those with a low *versus* high educational attainment, male *versus* female; and also for various definitions of employment *e.g.* any form of employment, full-time employment).

Algebraically, if $ER_{k,t}$ is the employment rate t years after education of category k, the expected number of years in employment after D years is given by

$$EYE_{k,D} = ER_{k,1}*D + (ER_{k,2} - ER_{k,1})*(D-1) + ...+ (ER_{k,D} - ER_{k,D-1})*1$$

Opting for a window of five years is arbitrary but it has been used here as a "reasonable" approximation of the length of the school-to-work transition process.

Figure 1.11. **Expected number of years spent in employment during the five years after leaving school,[a] by educational attainment, Denmark, Europe and Australia, 2007[b]**

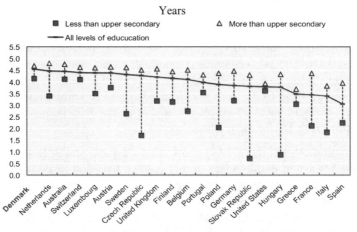

a) In the EULFS, individuals report on the year they have obtained their highest degree. Conditional on the respondent declaring he/she is no longer a student, this information is used to compute the durations underlying the indicator. In HILDA, respondents report on the number of years that have elapsed since they left full-time education. That information is used to compute durations, again conditional on the respondent declaring he/she is no longer a student.

b) 2006 for Australia.

Source: European Union Labour Force Survey (EULFS); and Melbourne Institute, Household, Income and Labour Dynamics in Australia Survey (HILDA), Release 6 for Australia.

Figure 1.12 conveys some additional information about the intensity of employment. It compares: *i)* the expected number of years in (any form and duration of) employment (reported in Figure 1.11); and *ii)* the expected number of years in full-time employment. Quite logically, for all countries examined, the expected time in full-time employment is lower. But Denmark is displaying a smaller drop than the other best achievers pointed out above: 0.7 years from 4.5 years (in employment) to 3.8 years (in full-time employment). The drop is of 1.6 years, 1.5 years, and 1.1 years respectively for the Netherlands, Australia and Switzerland.[26]

Figure 1.12. **Expected number of years spent in any employment *versus* full-time employment during the five years after leaving school,[a] by educational attainment, Denmark, Europe and Australia, 2007[b]**

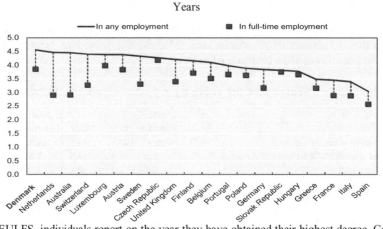

a) In the EULFS, individuals report on the year they have obtained their highest degree. Conditional on the respondent declaring he/she is no longer a student, this information is used to compute the durations underlying the indicator. In HILDA, respondents report on the number of years that have elapsed since they left full-time education. That information is used to compute durations, again conditional on the respondent declaring he/she is no longer a student.
b) 2006 for Australia.
Source: European Union Labour Force Survey (EULFS); and Melbourne Institute, Household, Income and Labour Dynamics in Australia (HILDA) Survey, Release 6 for Australia.

---

26.   The reader should bear in mind that our results are primarily driven by the cross-sectional incidence of full-time *versus* part-time contracts for individuals who left school up five years before *the moment of the interview*. If the EUFLS interview dates are not randomly distributed across the 12 months forming a post-schooling spell, this might lead to some under/overestimation of the incidence of part-time contracts. We assume indeed that a respondent who declares (potentially on month 12) that they are a permanent worker at the time of the interview has never had a part-time contract before. Conversely, we assume that someone with a part-time contract (on, for instance, month 1) will keep it until the end of the year spell.

3. Key points

The Danish youth unemployment rate (15-24) remained quite low over the past decade and constantly stayed significantly below the EU and OECD averages (Table 1.1). Before the recent economic downturn, the incidence of long-term unemployment was also extremely low by international standards. In 2008, it represented only 6.4% of the total Danish youth unemployment, while it accounted for 23.9% and 18.8% of the total in, respectively, Europe and the OECD.

Exposure to the labour market in Denmark starts early. Many young Danes enter the labour market when they are still studying. In 2008, the incidence of jobs among students aged 23-24 at 70% was just below the Dutch rate of 71% known to be one of the highest in Europe.

There remain structural concerns however. One of them is the relative situation of children of immigrants. Mid-2000s, they had poorer labour market outcomes than children of natives.

Table 1.1.   **Scoreboard for youth aged 15-24,[a] Denmark, 1998 and 2008**

	1998			2008		
	Denmark	EU[b]	OECD[b]	**Denmark**	EU[b]	OECD[b]
Employment rate (% of the age group)	**66.4**	40.1	44.5	**68.5**	39.4	43.9
Unemployment rate (UR) (% of the labour force)	**7.2**	17.1	14.8	**7.2**	15.0	13.2
Relative UR youth/adult (15-24)/(25-54)	**1.6**	2.2	2.4	**3.2**	2.8	2.8
Unemployment to population ratio (% of the age group)	**5.1**	7.7	7.1	**5.3**	6.4	6.1
Incidence of long-term unemployment (% of unemployment)	**8.1**	28.6	21.8	**6.4**	23.9	18.8
Incidence of temporary work (% of employment)	**27.2**	31.1	29.2	**23.0**	37.2	35.4
Incidence of part-time work (% of employment)	**45.5**	17.1	20.5	**55.7**	21.3	24.8
Neither in education nor in employment rate (% of the age group)[c]	**4.2**	13.1	13.4	**6.0**	10.2	11.2
School drop-outs (% of the age group)[d,e]	**8.2**	13.9	16.7	**15.2**	11.7	14.4
Relative UR low skills/high skills (<ISCED3)/(>ISCED3)[d]	**0.9**	2.5	2.4	**1.2**	2.1	2.2

ISCED 3: International standard classification of education referring to upper secondary education; LTU: long-term unemployment; NEET: neither in education nor in employment or training; UR: unemployment rate.

a)   16-24 for Iceland, Norway (1998 only), Spain, Sweden, the United Kingdom and the United States.
b)   Unweighted averages for the 19 OECD and EU countries and for the 30 OECD countries.
c)   2001 and 2007.
d)   1997 and 2006.
e)   School drop-outs are estimated by the share of youth not in education and without an upper secondary education.

Source: National labour force surveys; and *OECD Education database.*

It also takes quite a long time for young Danes to complete initial education and properly enter the labour market. More than 24% of young Danes still declare being student while aged 25-29, a higher share than elsewhere in Europe and the rest of the OECD, that, other things being equal, does not translate into achieving more human capital.

However, the overall assessment remains predominantly positive. For most Danish youth the transition from school to work is rather smooth. Indicators gathered in this chapter suggest that Denmark has a better performance than most OECD countries in this respect. And it is noteworthy that the performance gap between highly- and low-educated youth is lower than in most other countries examined.

Finally, the reader should bear in mind that Denmark's economy and labour market have been strong over the past decade. Such a favourable economic context has probably contributed a lot to the positive youth labour market outcomes highlighted here. However, the magnitude of the current economic crisis implies that the short-term future of youth employment is much more uncertain.

CHAPTER 2

INITIAL EDUCATION AND ON-THE-JOB TRAINING

Good-quality initial education is crucial in facilitating the transition from school to work and putting youth on a successful career track. Also, on-the-job training at the beginning of active life allows young people to fill the gaps in school-based education and acquire the skills required by firms.

The Danish public authorities recognise the importance of initial education and its relevance to labour market requirements. It has introduced several measures to enhance the effectiveness of its education system known for being one of the best funded in the world. A number of these measures address the drop-out problem, *i.e.* the relatively low propensity of Danish youth to complete upper secondary education.

This chapter looks at whether the Danish education and training system gives young people a good start in the labour market. Section 1 reviews the institutional arrangements. Section 2 presents different performance indicators on the education system. Section 3 focuses on strategies to improve performance. Section 4 discusses what is available for young people to acquire practical work-based or work-related skills or experience while in school. The final section reviews young adults' participation in on-the-job training.

1. The provision of education services

Denmark has a long tradition of private schooling and local (*i.e.* municipal) control of education, now embedded in a quasi-market that allocates public funds from the central government to various providers, *via* a *taximeter* system. That is the Danish version of the school voucher (see Box 2.1).

Box 2.1. **The taximeter or the Danish version of the voucher system**

In Denmark, schools receive public funding according to the number of pupils/students enrolled. The latter are free to choose their school.

This began in about 1990 and has spread to most school levels. The activity-based allocation system – or taximeter – was introduced gradually starting with the Open University in 1990, upper secondary technical colleges and business colleges in 1991, private primary and lower secondary schools in 1992, higher education in 1994, adult vocational training centres in 1995 and folk high schools and production schools in 1996.

Prior to the reforms, traditional and centralised state management of most financial and administrative matters characterised the organisation of educational institutions. Today, funds are allocated as grants by the central government to institutions based on the actual levels of pupil/student activity, objectively measured in full-time semesters or years. All courses are given a politically-determined rate, published annually in the government's finance bill. To ease administration and facilitate transparency, the system only contains a limited number of rate categories. Consequently, institutions have gained significant powers over financial as well as administrative management, including decisions on: *i)* intake of pupils to specific education programmes and/or courses *ii)* planning and organisation of teaching activities; and *iii)* planning and organisation of work.

The taximeter system comprises four elements of grants: *i)* a basic grant; *ii)* a teaching grant; *iii)* an operational grant; and iv) a building grant to cover rent, interest, debt servicing and maintenance. Except for the basic grant (which is a lump-sum grant irrespective of the size of the institution, covering basic operational expenses), all grants are activity-determined. The actual grant depends on student numbers, age distribution of pupils, and the seniority of teachers.

Source: Patrinos (2001).

A child can begin compulsory education at the earliest by the age of five but he/she must begin education at the latest in the calendar year when they reach the age of six. Danish children have today ten years of compulsory education (from six to 16), since pre-school class has recently been made compulsory (Figure 2.1).

Compulsory education can take place through:

- Enrolment in public schools, free of charge;
- Enrolment in private schools with a substantial financial support by the state (typically 80% of total costs);
- Or even teaching at home under the supervision of the local school authorities.[27]

---

27.   In Denmark, education but not schooling is mandatory. Parents have long been free to educate their children as they see fit including through home schooling.

Figure 2.1.   **The Danish education system: an overview**

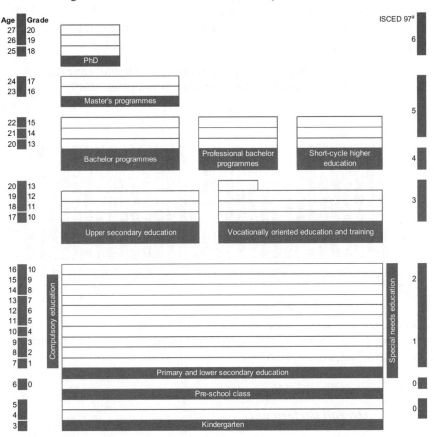

a)   International Standard Classification of Education.

Source: Danish Ministry of Education (2008).

Denmark has an educational system that is predominantly general until the end of compulsory education at the age of 16. Pupils follow the same, relatively undifferentiated, curriculum. At age 16, children branch off to a wide number of alternative routes. About half remain for a voluntary tenth year, with the other half going straight to upper secondary education, where schools are either general academic, or vocational preparing students for particular professions. The transition from basic school (primary and lower secondary) to so-called "youth education" (upper secondary), at the end of compulsory education is a crucial moment in a young person's educational career.

Today, any group of parents can claim public funding by declaring themselves a private school if they have at least 28 students.

At the age of 16, vocational options emerge (Figure 2.1). About 48% of young people who stay on in education beyond the age of 16 opted in 2007 in Denmark for VET programmes, a proportion close to the OECD average (Figure 2.2).

Figure 2.2.　**Enrolment in general *versus* vocational*ᵃ* education in upper secondary education, OECD countries,*ᵇ* 2007**

Percentages

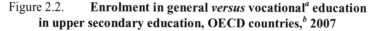

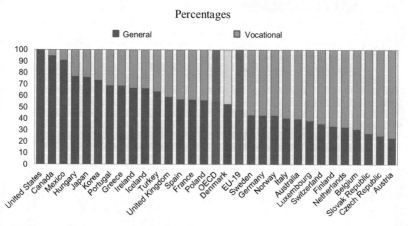

a)　Includes the so-called pre-vocational education.
b)　Data for New Zealand are not available. Unweighted EU and OECD averages of countries shown.
Source: OECD (2009a), *Education at a Glance.*

2. Performance of the education system

A.　*Overall performance*

Denmark shows a relatively poor performance in terms of its school drop-out[28] rate. The proportion of its youth population aged 20-24 with no upper secondary education reached 18.6 % in 2008, which is slightly

---

28.　　What is actually meant by the term "drop-out"? Educators tend to consider someone as a "drop-out" if s/he interrupts his/her upper secondary education before passing the final exams and obtaining the diploma. The definition used in this report is slightly different. It basically refers to the highest qualification that youth (15-24) or young adults (20-24) eventually obtain. Although the typical upper secondary school student will finish his/her secondary education by the age of 18, some do not, for a variety of reasons. Estimations of drop-out rates based on the attainment of groups that are relatively young might count as a "drop-out" someone taking a temporary break from his/her schooling. However, by the time a person is 20-24, much of the opportunity for completing upper secondary qualifications has gone. As a consequence, the drop-out rate is defined here as the share of 20-24-year-olds who are not attending school and who have not obtained an ISCED 3 qualification.

above the OECD average (Figure 2.3). However, it is well above the proportion of 6-7% recorded in central European countries, namely Poland, the Slovak Republic and the Czech Republic or other Nordic countries like Sweden (9.5%) or Finland (10.2%). The Danish government is committed to reducing drastically the number of school drop-outs in the next years having decided that in 2015, 95% of each youth cohort should attain at least upper secondary education.[29] For the OECD (see OECD, 2009f), this official target may be unrealistic and may need to be revised in order to realistically take account of certain types of vocational education not currently included.

Figure 2.3.   **School drop-outs[a] among youth aged 20-24, selected OECD countries,[b] 2008[c]**

Percentages

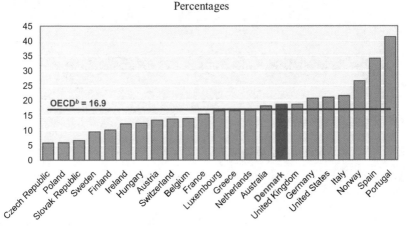

a)   No longer in education without ISCED 3.
b)   Unweighted average of countries shown.
c)   2006 for Australia.
Source: EULFS, and Melbourne Institute Household, Income and Labour Dynamics in Australia (HILDA), Release 6 for Australia.

The share of young adults aged 25-34 with a tertiary education (*i.e.* holding an ISCED 5/6 qualification) at 40% in 2007 is well above the OECD average of 34%. But it is inferior to what is observed in Canada, Korea or Japan

---

29.   This target was established in the 2006 Danish government's strategy Progress, Innovation and Cohesion. It is based on the so-called "profile model" which estimates the theoretical completion rate 25 years after leaving compulsory education, given behaviour and transition frequencies across the education system and age groups in a given year. Immigrants are only included if having arrived in the country at age 15 or before. The rate achieved in 2006-07 was 83%.

(Figure 2.4). A good point is that graduation rates are on the rise – younger cohorts reach ISCED 5/6 more systematically than older ones – but not as much as in countries like Korea, Japan, France, Ireland or Spain.

Figure 2.4.   **Proportion of 25-34-year-olds with tertiary qualification, OECD countries, 2007**

Percentages

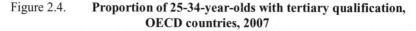

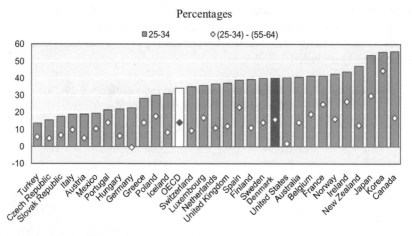

Source: OECD Education database.

B.   *Achievement at age 15*

Poor PISA results given the country generous public funding of education

Test scores from PISA[30] 2003 revealed a mixed average performance for Danish teenagers. And that performance was largely confirmed by the PISA 2006 average test scores (Figure 2.5). A mixed assessment of performance also applies for low and high achievers (*i.e.* 1st and 3rd quartiles respectively, Figure 2.5). In all three cases, Denmark occupies a position that is very close to the OECD average.

These results need be considered in the light of: *i)* the country relatively high GDP per head; and *ii)* its very generous public funding of education.[31] The latter absorbed 4.4% of GDP in 2006, well above the OECD average of 3.7 % (OECD, 2009a).

---

30.   The OECD's Programme for International Student Assessment.

31.   Primary, secondary and post-secondary non-tertiary education from public and private sources.

Figure 2.5.   **Danish students' performance, based on PISA 2006, OECD countries**

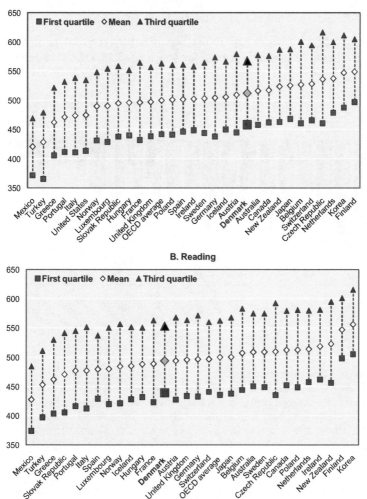

A. Mathematics

B. Reading

Source: OECD PISA 2006 database.

PISA scores suggest immigrants' children are lagging behind

It is particularly important to pay attention to what happens within the educational system for the children of immigrants, as a gap at that (early) stage of individuals' career may contribute to labour market integration problems.

Figure 2.6 displays the relative performance of children of immigrants in PISA 2006 test scores in mathematics.[32] Children of immigrant origin are doing less well at school than natives. The gap in Denmark is lower than in Belgium or France, but much larger than in Australia, Canada, New Zealand, the United States and the United Kingdom.

Figure 2.6.   **Score gap^a in mathematics between natives and first-or second-generation immigrants^b for youth aged 15, OECD countries, 2006**

Points

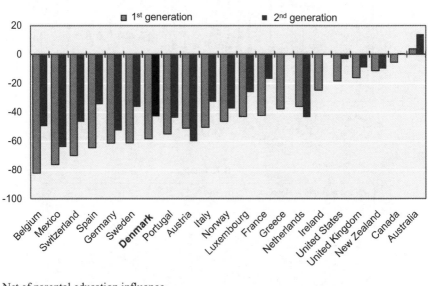

a)   Net of parental education influence.

b)   In PISA native students are those students born in the country of assessment or who had at least one parent born in the country; second-generation students are those born in the country of assessment but whose parents were both born in another country; first-generation students are those students born outside the country of assessment and whose parents were also born in another country.

Source: OECD PISA 2006 database.

A recent OECD report highlights also that children of immigrants in Denmark, and particularly sons of immigrants, have a relatively high drop-out rate from secondary schools (Liebig and Widmaier, 2009). A little more than 50% of native-born sons of immigrants aged 20-29 not in education had less than upper secondary education in 2007, compared to 30% of sons of natives. The figures for daughters are 34% and 22%, respectively. These differences are among the highest in OECD countries.

---

32.   Theoretically less influenced by background variables than reading scores.

C.   Achievement beyond 16

Starting and completing tertiary education late

According to statistics from the Danish Ministry of Education, students in Denmark are rather old when they start and complete tertiary education and become fully available for the labour market (Table 2.1).

Table 2.1.   **Median age when starting an education and at graduation, Denmark, 2000 and 2005**

		2000	2005
Short-cycle higher education	Start	23.8	23.4
	Graduation	26.4	25.8
Professional bachelors	Start	23.8	23.7
	Graduation	27.7	27.3
Bachelors at universities	Start	21.8	21.6
	Graduation	25.0	25.2

Source: Danish Ministry of Education (2008), *Facts and Figures 2007.*

Indicators based on the European Survey on Income and Living Conditions (EUSILC) conveys the same message (Figure 2.7). Below the age of 20, the share of those who are in tertiary education in Denmark is negligible, lower than the European average, and much inferior to that observed in France – a country where most students immediately start tertiary education once upper secondary education is completed. Quite logically the share of tertiary education students older than 23 is higher in Denmark than elsewhere in Europe.

The issue at stake is not that Danes are more or less prone to participate in tertiary education. It is rather that they are older than their European peers when they enter tertiary education. Consequently, they are also older when they graduate. The latter is clearly visible when considering the actual age at which adults aged 30-35 in 2007 declare they graduated from tertiary education (Figure 2.8).

Figure 2.7.   **Individuals aged 17-30 attending tertiary education, Denmark, France and Europe, 2006**

Percentages*a*

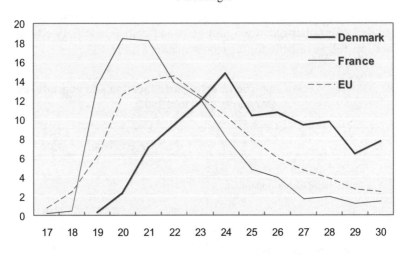

a)   Frequency distribution by year of age.

Source: European Survey on Income and Living Conditions (EUSILC).

Figure 2.8.   **Age at which degree was obtained for adults 30-35 in possession of an upper secondary (ISCED 3) or tertiary (>ISCED 3) degree, Denmark and Europe, 2007**

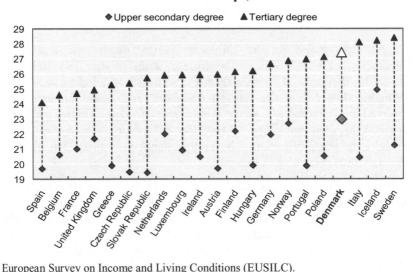

Source: European Survey on Income and Living Conditions (EUSILC).

As seen in Chapter 1, Denmark's large share of old students does not translate into achieving more human capital (Figure 1.7). Finishing studies later reduces lifetime earnings as the person has fewer years to use the acquired skills on the labour market, but much of this loss is supported by public finances (*via* foregone tax revenue), whereas the person gets all the intangible benefits of "student life" which for natural reasons are untaxed. Many argue however that older students in Denmark have accumulated significant labour market experience as many hold student jobs, which may help them have a smoother and faster school-to-work transition.

Determinants of late completion

There is no doubt that late completion is partially the consequence of late entrance into tertiary education. Most of this delay is due to long waits before beginning to study, as many young people in Denmark take the voluntary 10th grade,[33] work in a café, travel abroad or enjoy their time in other ways while considering what to do in life (OECD, 2006b).

Another factor is the allocation mechanism within tertiary education. It seems that most Danes who enter into tertiary education start at university but then – when confronted with difficulties – gradually reorient themselves towards shorter (and presumably less demanding) programmes. Although access to tertiary education is conditional on having good marks at the end of upper secondary education, the existing evidence suggests that accessing university is relatively easy in Denmark. But enrolment does not automatically lead to graduation. About a third of those who start such a programme drop out at some stage (Danish Ministry of Education, 2008), generally to start another programme, with the consequence that those who eventually graduate from short programmes or vocational qualifications in tertiary education are older than those who manage to stay at university (Table 2.1).

The two following results, discontinued tertiary education and programme reorientation, point at poor matching between individuals' selection of studies and their capabilities, as well as at insufficient preparation for further studies for lower levels of education (*i.e.* poor performance at the age of 15 in core topics highlighted by PISA). A more direct selection and assignment mechanism at the entrance of tertiary education would definitely contribute to lowering the age upon graduation.

Another point is that Denmark offers relatively generous and flexible education grants and loans to all its students aged 18 or more (see Box 2.2

---

33. A voluntary extra year of lower secondary education before the student enters an upper secondary programme. These so-called "bridge-building" programmes are meant to facilitate transition from lower to upper secondary education programme.

for more information on these schemes). Evidence based on EUSILC displayed in Figure 2.9 suggests that this parameter plays a key role in extending the duration of studies. Across Europe, the larger the amount directly[34] transferred to students, the older the age upon graduation.

Box 2.2. **Education grants and loans in Denmark**

Every Dane over the age of 18 is entitled to public support for his or her further education (only tested against parental income for youth not attending tertiary education and aged less than 20). Tuition at Danish public and most private educational institutions is free for Danish students and for all EU/EEA students as well as for students participating in an exchange programme. Student support is granted by the state (in the form of state education grants and loans), conditional on students attending institutions and programmes approved by the Ministry of Education.

Support for students' living costs is awarded by the State Education Grant and Loan Scheme), a system managed by the Danish Educational Support Agency in collaboration with educational institutions and under the auspices of the Danish Ministry of Education.

Financial characteristics

The maximum amounts awarded in 2008 for education grants are as follows:

- Students living with their parents: EUR 343 (DKK 2 574) per month.
- Students living on their own: EUR 690 (DKK 5 177) per month.

Both categories of students can obtain state loans worth EUR 340 (DKK 2 562) per month.

Over 300 000 Danes benefit from education grants and state loans every year. The 2008 budget amounts around 0.8% of GDP.

Education grants and loans (and study abroad scholarships) are paid to a *NemKonto* in monthly instalments. A *NemKonto* is an ordinary bank account which the student already has and which the public authorities use when they pay out money.

On completion of their studies, students must start paying back the state loans. Repayment must begin one year after the end of the year in which they have completed their studies. The duration of the period of repayment must not exceed 15 years. About half of all students make use of state loans.

During the period of study, state loans will carry a 4% annual interest. On completion of the studies, the annual interest rate is the discount rate of the Danish Central Bank plus an adjustment which can be negative or positive, but at most plus 1 percentage point.

---

34. Indirect transfers *via* family credit-taxes or child allowances are left aside.

Until students are 20, education grants depend upon parental income. When that exceeds a certain amount the grants are reduced on a sliding scale, ending in a minimum grant. Beyond the age of 20, only the student's own income matters. It should not exceed EUR 10 190 (DKK 76 440) per year (2008 limit). Students who overstep that limit have to repay some of the grants and loans received that year plus 7%. However they have the option of not accepting state support for a period of time thus preserving their rights.

Main rules

Altogether the rules make for a flexible system. Students have the option of organising their studies according to their personal preferences and earning possibilities. At the same time, however, they incur a measure of personal accountability for managing their financial situation.

Youth over 18 attending youth education (i.e. a general or vocational upper secondary education programme)

They must attend classes, sit examinations and in other ways demonstrate that they are active in their educational programmes. No time limits are placed on this type of support. Students are eligible for support for any number of courses, with the exception of certain upper secondary programmes.

Students over 18 enrolled in tertiary education

They are entitled to a number of monthly grants corresponding to the prescribed duration of the chosen study, plus 12 months. Inside a maximum of 70 grants students can change from one course to another.

Students in tertiary education (under a time limitation) have the choice of using these grants later, either to prolong their studies (for instance, to prepare for re-examination after a failed exam) or under certain circumstances to obtain double grants for a period of time at the end of their studies.

Extra monthly grants

In particular situations – mainly sickness and childbirth – students can apply for extra monthly grants. New mothers are eligible for 12 and new fathers for six extra monthly grants, with certain stipulations.

Support for studies abroad

Danes can obtain support for studies abroad. Courses of study have to meet the same conditions for recognition as Danish ones. For studies in the Nordic countries, support is awarded for the prescribed duration of the chosen study, plus 12 months. For studies in other foreign countries, students are supported for four-year courses or for the last four years of longer ones. Danish grants can be used to finance studies abroad when they are accepted as part of a study programme at a Danish institution.

Source: Danish Ministry of Education, *www.sustyrelsen.dk/index.html?/in_english/default.html.*

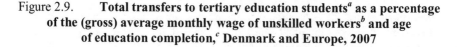

Figure 2.9.   **Total transfers to tertiary education students[a] as a percentage of the (gross) average monthly wage of unskilled workers[b] and age of education completion,[c] Denmark and Europe, 2007**

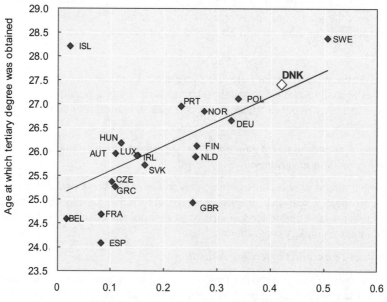

Total transfers as a percentage of low-skilled gross youth wage

a)   Aged 15-29 who declare being primarily students and possess at least an ISCED 3 degree.
b)   Aged 15-29 without ISCED 3.
c)   Age highest degree was obtained among 30-35-year-olds.
Source: European Survey on Income and Living Conditions (EUSILC).

Finally, the (gross) wage premium associated with holding a tertiary degree is one of the lowest in OECD countries (OECD, 2009a). What is more, given Denmark's (high) progressivity of income taxation, this probably means that the net rate of return is one of the lowest in Europe. But contrary to education grants and other monetary transfers, this parameter does not seem to be strongly correlated with the speed at which students pursue their studies (Figure 2.10).

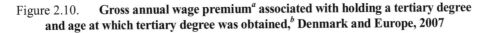

Figure 2.10.   **Gross annual wage premium^a associated with holding a tertiary degree and age at which tertiary degree was obtained,^{b} Denmark and Europe, 2007**

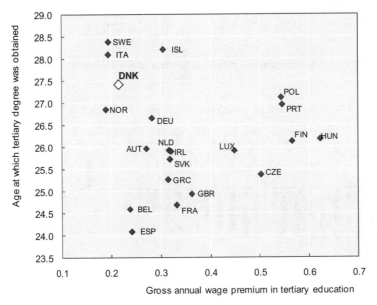

Gross annual wage premium in tertiary education

a)   Estimated model is a Mincerian equation when the education variable is categorical (ref=ISCED 3 or upper secondary education).

b)   Among adults aged 30-35.

Source: European Survey on Income and Living Conditions (EUSILC).

3. Strategies to improve educational attainment

A.   *Continuing to develop learning activities in kindergarten*

There is a growing recognition that quality pre-school provides young children, particularly those from low-income or other disadvantaged backgrounds, with a good start in life (OECD, 2006a). Participation in pre-school – where children are exposed to an actual educational content – could be particularly good for the latter, as it could reduce the incidence of dropping out from school or act as a long term catalyst of school-to-work transition.

A relatively unknown feature of the PISA 2003 survey is that participants were asked to report their pre-school experience before they started primary schooling. This information can be used to measure the correlation between early education and cognitive achievement at the age of 15 (that, in itself, is a good predictor of future academic and professional success). In Denmark, reported score differences (Figure 2.11) between those who spent two years or more in kindergarten and those who spent no time range from 14 to 16 points on the PISA scale (or 0.14 to 0.16 of a standard deviation).[35] The score gaps in Denmark, for both reading and mathematics, are close to the equivalent OECD average.

Figure 2.11.   **Kindergarten non-attendance and score gap[a] at the age of 15, OECD countries,[b] 2003**

No attendance *versus* two or more years of attendance[c]

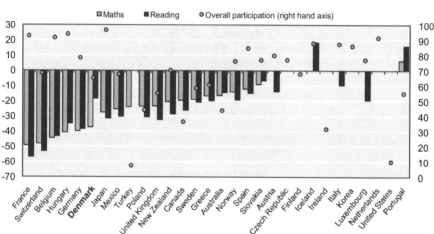

a)   Ordinary least squares (OLS) coefficients not statistically significant at the 5% level are set to zero. The regression includes the following control variables: mother education, father education, immigration status, index of socio-economic and cultural status.
b)   Unweighted average for OECD countries.
c)   Reference group.
Source: OECD PISA 2003 database.

Those who legitimately fear that these results remain potentially spurious should consider that they accord with the evidence published in the research literature[36] that aims at measuring the causal benefits of early education.

---

35.   The reported coefficients are *net* of what should logically be attributed to background variables that are beyond the control of education and social policy. These variables include the level of education of parents (both mother and father), the immigration status, as well as the socio-economic and cultural status of the parents.

36.   Carneiro and Heckman (2003) review several evaluation studies of the long-term benefits of pre-school programmes on children from low-income families. Reviewed studies find evidence of sizeable long-term effects on school achievement and grade repeating, particularly when efforts are sustained beyond

International data (Figure 2.12) show that childcare attendance among children aged 3-5 is higher in Denmark (91.3%) than in many OECD countries.[37] But pre-school should not be amalgamated with childcare services. Childcare refers to arrangements made for the care of children when parents are not available. Traditionally, childcare has been viewed as a tool to foster (mainly female) employment and support families, rather than being part of the education system. Pre-schools, by contrast, are supposed to offer a range of educational and developmental programmes to children, delivered by staff with teaching qualifications. As mentioned earlier, there is abundant evidence, from the evaluation literature concerning the long-term benefits of pre-school (*i.e.* school-like learning approaches). The evaluation of the outcomes of child-care programmes are much more contrasted, and sometimes negative (Lefèbvre *et al.*, 2006).

Figure 2.12.   **Pre-school attendance rates among 3-5-year-olds in OECD countries, 2007**

Percentages

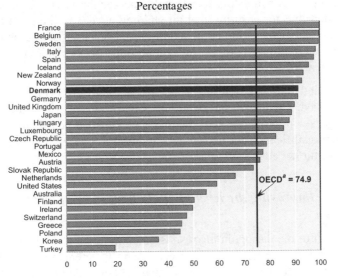

a)   Unweighted average of countries shown.

Source: OECD Education database.

the pre-school period. Positive effects of pre-school education on being on grade and school completion have been found in France, where pre-school is almost universal among 3-5-year-olds (Caille and Rosenwald, 2006). Boocock (1995) reviews childcare in Sweden and concludes that participation in pre-school has benefits in terms of cognitive development and school success, and that these are more positive for children of low-income families.

37.   The latest figures provided by the Ministry of Interior and Social Affairs, point at an even higher attendance rate of 96.6 % for the 3-5-year-olds in 2008.

In Denmark, services for children aged 0-6 have traditionally been considered as an integral part of the social welfare system (OECD, 2006a) and not of the education system. As a consequence, kindergarten and pre-school class have been more focused on psycho-social development more than learning. The Ministry of Interior and Social Affairs has the primary responsibility for national early childhood policy, although many policy and operational matters have for long been decentralised to local authorities. Indeed, the close monitoring of kindergartens takes place at municipal level, where teams of pedagogical advisors monitor font-line services and provide support to improve the quality of services.

The traditional division between childcare/kindergarten and primary education is currently reconsidered in Denmark following the 2007 legislative initiatives of the Danish Act of Day Care.[38] In particular, in the day-care facility or elsewhere in each locality, offering a language assessment test is mandatory for all children aged three. The local council is also responsible for ensuring that all children aged 3 in the local authority are offered language stimulating activities and other assistance as required, such as counselling parents for supporting their children's language development.

Qualified staff is key in the 2007 Act of Day Care. Most kindergarten facilities have a manager and deputy-manager, both of whom are qualified pedagogues. Up to 60% of staff members are certified pedagogues. And the minimum qualification for pedagogues requires 3.5 years at tertiary level in centres of further education.

B.   Improving the level of attainment in compulsory education

In light of the disappointing results on educational attainment, a number of measures have been taken in recent years to strengthen the education content of the earliest years in the formal school system. In particular, the introductory year for 6-year-olds has been made compulsory. The still unsatisfactory 2006 PISA results should convince the Danish authorities of

---

38.   The general purpose of early childhood education and care as specified by the 2007 Act of Day Care is to further the well-being, development and independence of children in consultation with their parents, while also functioning for educational, social and care purposes. All day care facilities have to make a learning plan, which describe how the day care works with six themes: personal and social competences, language, motor development, culture and nature. Each year, the work with the learning plan has to be evaluated and sent to the local authority for further discussion and action if necessary.

the necessity of continuing to strengthen the curriculum in primary and lower secondary schools. Extensive reforms are being implemented in the primary and lower secondary schools with the aim of improving the level of attainment in particular in core topics. The government has established in 2006 a new national agency for quality assurance and evaluation in compulsory education.

In April 2006, the Danish Parliament decided to make national tests a compulsory pedagogic tool in compulsory education. As part of the process of evaluating the students' learning outcomes, a range of obligatory national tests have been introduced. The tests[39] are designed by the Agency for quality assurance and evaluation of primary and lower secondary education. They are used to follow the individual student's acquisition of knowledge and skills so that the education process can be planned to a greater extent according to the individual student's strengths, weaknesses and potential.

The main purpose of the testing system is to provide teachers with a pedagogical tool to help them analyse the proficiency level of their pupils and the level of their class (Wandall, 2009). In order to reduce the incentive to "teaching to the test" and as precautionary measures against ranking of teachers, schools or local communities, it is forbidden by law to publish the items and the test results. Any test result obtained by a pupil, and even an average by a group of pupils, classes, schools or municipalities are strictly confidential.

Only those, who for professional reasons need information about the results, are allowed to see them. The teacher, for instance, has access to detailed reports with information about the individual pupils' result as well as test results on class level. The headmaster is allowed to see the pupil's overall results, the class results and the results for the school. The local government/municipalities have access to aggregate results of the individual schools. But the general public and the parents are not informed.

Developing standardised tests a as tool that professionals can use to gauge the results of their action is certainly a step in the right direction. It creates an environment in which school, teachers and municipalities supposedly pay more attention to the determinants of children's attainment. There are also good reasons for preventing individual raw scores to be disseminated. One of them is simply that gaps between raw scores are unlikely to reflect teaching quality differentials exclusively, as it is well established that final scores are also driven by non-uniformly distributed

---

39.   Danish students must complete the following ten tests: Danish, with a focus on reading in grades 2, 4, 6 and 8; English in grade 7; Mathematics in grades 3 and 6; Geography in grade 8; Biology in grade 8; and Physics/chemistry in grade 8.

socioeconomic background factors. But is it so clear that Denmark's very restrictive approach to results dissemination represents the best possible option? As mentioned earlier, any form of ranking based on test scores is in principle banned from the Danish scheme. What is more, it contains no element of school accountability as there are no consequences, such as monetary awards or takeover threats, attached to school performance. Continued efforts are needed to build a culture of evaluation. Ensuring contestability in carrying out the performance of teaching and schools might yield quality gains, according to OECD (2009f).

C.   Combating late tertiary study start and completion

Previous sections of this report contain abundant evidence that young Danes are already quite old when they undertake tertiary education (Table 2.1). Most of this delay is due to long waits between lower secondary (making the end of compulsory attendance) and upper secondary education. Incidentally, it is worth stressing that these waits probably increase the risk of dropping out from studies.

For instance, public spending on the voluntary 10th grade could be better employed elsewhere in the education system to speed up entry into further studies. As many as 30% of the students attending the 10th grade are thought to be already academically ready for further education and many more would have been with further guidance during secondary school. Recent reforms of the 10th grade (for 16-year-olds) have strengthened its educational content and provided opportunities for students to try out vocational education pathways to help them make better career and study choices. The Labour Market Commission's final report, released in August 2009, recommends that the 10th grade should be targeted more carefully at students who are not capable of completing further study without extra help (Labour Market Commission, 2009).[40]

A similar phenomenon is observed at the articulation between upper secondary education and tertiary education. What is more, within tertiary education, Danish students frequently change study course, with the mechanical implication that they tend to be older when they properly start the programme they will eventually graduate from.

Addressing this problem is a challenging endeavour as there is not simple answer to a phenomenon so evidently deeply rooted in the Danish

---

40.   The Labour Market Commission was established in 2007 to provide recommendations on how to achieve the employment goals required by the government's 2015 Plan for fiscal policy.

culture. Possible options include: *i)* a better command of core skills at the end of compulsory education in order to increase the level of "study readiness" of teenagers; *ii)* improved guidance within schools; and probably also *iii)* financial incentives to start the next level of education earlier.

Regarding financial incentives, it is hard to say exactly how much these matter for educational choices. However, there is evidence (Figure 2.9) that across Europe the generosity of student financial assistance is correlated with the duration of studies.

The Danish government proposed in 2006 a set of adjustments of the public education grants with the explicit aim of enticing youth to start and complete tertiary education earlier. The proposals comprised : *i)* a EUR 130 (DKK 1 000) cut of the monthly education grant for living costs for those starting more than two years after completing secondary education;[41] *ii)* for all students, EUR 130 (DKK 1 000) of the monthly education grant retained and paid out as a bonus at the end of each semester conditional on sufficient progress; *iii)* abolition of the right to 12 months of extra education grants in excess of the stipulated programme duration; and *iv)* removal of the possibility to "save" education grant payments for use after the stipulated programme duration.

However, the final decision was much more limited in scope. In the 2006 Welfare Agreement, the single most important change for a student was an easier access to tertiary education if he/she enters tertiary education within two years of completing secondary school. Starting from the 2009 enrolment, students entering tertiary education will have their grade average multiplied by a factor of 1.08 and thereby will have easier access to studies where the number of study places is limited by a *numerus clausus*. But this is unlikely to fundamentally affect students. In Denmark, open access exists to most university (ISCED 5A) programmes, except in certain specialised ones which are mainly intended for professional bachelors[42] (Eurydice, 2007). In addition, reflecting lower demographics, the number of available places in these areas now seems to exceed the number of applicants (OECD, 2005b).

The Labour Market Commission again proposed to introduce financial incentives to encourage earlier completion of education. It recommends paying a tax-free bonus of DKK 10 000 to students who complete their first

---

41. And the right to larger student loans in exchange.

42. Graduates in teacher training for primary and lower secondary education, and in other fields of study such as social services, business and administration, and engineering.

year of tertiary vocational study within three years after completing upper secondary education. It also recommends terminating the current practice of giving education grants for one year longer than the specified duration of a course, for students starting tertiary education two years after finishing upper secondary school.

Measures aimed at changing the attitude of providers (*i.e.* tertiary education institutions) were also announced in the 2006 Welfare Agreement. New financing structures will bring actual study times better in line with scheduled study times. The intention is also that part of the public financing will be paid out when students complete exams (Danish Ministry of Finance, 2006). From 2009, the bonus that universities receive when students complete a bachelor programme is conditional on the duration of the study. The universities will receive a bachelor bonus when students complete a bachelor programme within the prescribed study period plus one year and master's bonus when students complete a master's programme within the prescribed study period.

These are steps in the right direction. But other decisions could prove counterproductive. For instance, the 2007 decision to rise earnings ceilings under the very generous public grants for student's living cost allow students to earn more while still receiving full education grants and may indeed delay study completion. Research finds that the higher the individual's own earnings while studying, the longer it takes to complete studies (Gupta and An, 2005).

4. Between school and work

A.   *Orientation, guidance and placement*

Good career education and guidance, prior to young people's entry into the labour market, is widely recognised in the literature as being one of the elements fostering a smooth school-to-work transition (Ryan, 1999; OECD, 2004a). In the Danish context, study guidance also appears as a potential catalyst of the speed of transition between the different levels of education and an element that could reduce initial education's duration and school drop-outs.

There are also reasons to believe that study and career counselling provided by schools is particularly important in the vocational stream for pupils who do not learn from their families or other well-connected social networks, when they have to opt for a particular VET programme, as is the case for many in Denmark. Finally, the changing nature of labour market needs also matter and justify paying intention to guidance.

Guidance after school-leaving[43]

Youth guidance centres have a mandate to reach out to drop-outs aged less than 25. Their main role is to help these get back into the educational system. The youth guidance centres must offer guidance and assistance to any youth who "has completed compulsory education, is less than 25-year-olds, has not completed an upper secondary education or a higher education or is not currently studying one of these".

Guidance within schools

On August 1st 2004, a simpler and more transparent guidance system was enacted. Whereas the former system was based on guidance services provided by teachers working part-time as guidance counsellors, guidance is now delivered by the staff of the youth guidance centres.

It starts in grade 6 and continues until grade 10 (end of lower secondary education). From grade 9, career guidance also consists of bridge-building schemes that offer students the possibility to familiarise themselves with the demands of upper secondary education programmes. A personal education portfolio follows each student into upper secondary education and serves as basis for talks about future career planning.

The Ministry of Education and the Ministry of Employment have decided in November 2009 to focus on targeted measures for the 15-17-year-olds. All primary school pupils will prepare an education plan in collaboration with their parents, the school and the youth guidance centre The plan should lead to further education or should describe what the young person will otherwise doing. The education plan may include activities such as education, employment, internship, stay abroad or volunteer work. If pupils do not follow their education plan, their parents will risk losing child benefits.

Additional resources have also been provided for increased co-operation between youth guidance centres, educational institutions and the Public Employment Service (PES). The Ministry of Education and the Ministry of Employment will co-operate to develop a database, which will ensure a full overview of the education and training of each young individual. This will enable a quick identification of vulnerable young people and provide the information needed to offer a targeted effort.

---

43.   See also Box 4.4.

B.   *Vocational education and training (VET) system*

Organisation

The VET system encompasses programmes of durations ranging from 18 months to 5.5 years that are divided into two parts: a "basic course", which is broad in its scope and a "main course", in which the trainee specialises within a craft or a trade and signs an apprenticeship contract with a firm. The basic course consists of both compulsory and optional subjects. The optional subjects provide the individual trainee with the possibility of acquiring additional qualifications in regard to either the main course or to gain access to further or higher education. The length of the basic course in the technical training programmes will vary from programme to programme, and from one trainee to the next.

Approximately one-third of a youth cohort enrols in a VET programme after completing lower secondary education. There is a long-term decrease in the number of young people who enter a VET programme as the trend over the past decades has been to opt for the more academically-oriented upper secondary education programmes (*Dansk Arbejdsgiverforening*, 2009).

However, access to this system intervenes often after the traditional gap years that young Danes grant themselves before undertaking an upper secondary qualification. The latter explains why in 2005 students were almost 21 years of age when starting VET (Danish Ministry of Education, 2008).

In Denmark, VET is thus organised in a sequential way: students first spend some time (ranging from 10 to 60 weeks) attending a class-based curriculum on a full-time basis (the so-called "basic course"), and then move on to (full-time) apprenticeships in firms for another two to three years (the so-called "main course"). In traditional dual systems – such as in Austria, Germany or Switzerland – school-based and work-based training are provided in parallel and involve an employment contract plus formal schooling – normally one and a half to two days per week.

A limited number (about 5%) of students choose an "apprenticeship-only" pathway into VET. The apprenticeship pathway constitutes an alternative, especially for practically-oriented trainees who are tired of school. In the apprenticeship pathway, the entire basic course is acquired by means of in-company training.

Denmark has also developed pre-vocational production schools.[44] Since 1978, these schools offer youth aged 16+ and who are not ready for the normal VET programme a practical or "production-related" learning environment. Students are offered the opportunity to participate in practical work in different areas ranging from metal, carpentry and textiles to media, theatre and music. Part of the basic course of the VET programme can be attended in production schools. There are also financial incentives to foster closer co-operation between VET and production schools.

Apprentice wages have a special regime. Within each sector, a minimum wage for apprentices is negotiated every third year in collective labour agreements. Additionally, the apprentice – as in an ordinary employment contract– has the opportunity to negotiate a higher salary. Firms receive important subsidies to hire and train apprentices. As a result, the average cost for an apprentice is half the cost for an ordinary employee. The wage received by an apprentice is however attractive for a young person, being 60% higher than the state education grant.

The VET system performs well for those who complete it

The VET system in Denmark has a strong "dual" component, synonymous with: *i)* systematic involvement of firms and social partners; and *ii)* (partially as a result of that) a high job-readiness for those who complete it (see Box 2.3 for a presentation of the principles on which it is based).

Most trainees enter VET *via* the basic course and then apply for an apprenticeship and to the main-course part. In fact, everybody who has completed lower secondary education can be admitted to the basic course but a contract with an enterprise is required in order to continue on the main course. The internal drop-out rate is, however, high. Only around 70% of new students complete the basic course and 80% the main course. Many of the trainees who drop out continue in other VET programmes or in the general upper secondary education programmes. Nonetheless, 40% of all drop-outs are estimated not to continue any education or training programme within the next ten years. The drop-out rate is higher among men than women and higher among immigrants than among those with Danish origin (National Education Authority, 2008). Reducing the number of trainees dropping out is an important political priority.

---

44.   The *Korsor* production school was presented as a good practice in 1999 by the OECD (OECD, 1999).

Box 2.3. **The VET system in Denmark**

The VET system includes four types of programmes: agricultural, commercial, social and health care, and technical. The system is part of the Danish youth education system, and as such, is primarily targeted at teenagers (16+). However, the average age of trainees in VET is 22, and the VET system also offers a wide range of possibilities for young adults (25+). Furthermore, the trend is towards an integration of initial VET and continuing VET in one system (see Box 2.5).

The VET system is based on three main principles:

The dual training principle

Periods in school alternating with periods of training in an enterprise. This principle ensures that the trainees acquire theoretical, practical, general and personal skills which are in demand by the labour market.

Social partner involvement

Social partners take part directly in the overall decision- making and daily running of the VET system.

Lifelong learning opportunities

The system is highly flexible, offering learners the possibility of taking part in a course now and returning to the VET system at a later point in time to add to their VET qualifications in order to access further and higher education. Furthermore, VET and continuing VET are integrated in order to ensure coherence between different qualifications and competence levels.

Source: National Education Authority (2008).

Another element is that the Danish VET system is relatively demanding. It takes on average four years to obtain a VET degree. It is also almost entirely up to the students to find a firm willing to take them as apprentices. Research also suggests that a good level of mathematics is the best passport to success in some VET programmes (National Education Authority, 2008).

Policy makers rightly concerned by the overall incidence of drop-outs are trying to improve the quality of VET. All VET schools in Denmark must now develop action plans aimed at increasing retention and all VET students must now have a "contact teacher" acting as a personal mentor/tutor. They also reformed VET in order to accommodate the needs of those forming the lower end of the skill distribution (*e.g.* more *flexication*,[45] shorter programmes lasting only 18 months and leading to "partial qualifications", less school-based education implying less time in the basic course before starting apprenticeship main course). The challenge, however, is to raise VET attendance and completion rates without compromising quality, in particular the willingness of firms to recruit, train and pay apprentices.

C.   Student work

In Denmark, the first work experience occurs well before students complete their initial education. This is due to a high incidence of student jobs, as highlighted in Chapter 1 (Figure 1.6).

Most economists would support the prediction that limited exposure to the labour market (*i.e.* less than 20 hours/week) during study years should be conducive to quicker and smoother school-to-work transition. The inherent search process involved in finding jobs while studying should help young people decide what they intend to do later (*i.e.* reduce search and matching costs). Moreover, some of the skills acquired on the job are likely to be transferable across employers and lift wages at a later stage. On the other hand, most of these jobs are potentially relatively poor in skill contents.

Whether student jobs are beneficial or not has been extensively researched in the United States. While some of the earlier studies (*e.g.* Greenberger and Steinberg 1986) tend to find negative impacts, others by Eckstein and Wolpin (1999), Oettinger (1999), and Ruhm (1997) show that far from being the case that all student work is detrimental, modest involvement in work activities while studying actually leads to positive outcomes. In particular, Ruhm (1997) finds strong evidence that early work experience leads to higher future wages and better fringe benefits. Additionally, he finds that students working ten hours per week during upper secondary schooling have a higher graduation probability than those who do not work at all, although heavier work (>20 hours/week) commitment is associated with a lower probability of graduation.

Another issue, particularly relevant in the Danish context, concerns the relationship between student worker and the overall duration of studies (see Section 2). Internationally, the topic has received little attention. What can be said for Denmark is that some researchers (Gupta and An, 2005) found evidence that the higher the individual's own earnings (*via* students jobs) while studying, the longer it takes to complete studies.

---

45.   "Flexication" is a key word in the Danish educational policy. It means that VET – and other forms of education – must be designed according to the needs of the user, to maximise his/her chance of success.

D.   Apprenticeships and training places in the current crisis

From 2003 to 2008, the number of apprenticeships increased by 39%, but fell between mid-2008 and mid-2009 due to the financial crisis. Subsequently, enrolment in school-based practical training programmes has increased substantially. A number of measures have been taken to support apprenticeships, including improving financial incentives for employers and training colleges' capacity to find internships and training places.

Many higher education courses require students to complete a compulsory work placement and it is feared that if students do not secure one, they will drop out of their studies. As a response to the current downturn, the government has announced in September 2009 that it will invest EUR 180 million (DKK 1.35 billion) in securing 5 000 internship places next year for students to prevent them joining the unemployment queue (Box 2.4).

Box 2.4. **5 000 additional apprenticeships and training places in 2010**

1 650 places in private companies. These internships are subsidised by the state through a cash bonus to the companies of EUR 800 (DKK 6 000) per month; this is 67% of the intern salary in the training period. After four and seven months the company will receive an additional bonus of EUR 2 150 (DKK 16 000).

1 500 places in schools in the following occupations: data and communications, electricians, mechanics, carpentry, technical designer and construction.

1 650 *places in regions and municipalities.* The government, the regions and the municipalities will propose a plan for internships before end of 2009.

200 places in the state, funded through an increase in Employment Minister allocated quotas.

There is no age restriction on the access to the 5 000 new places. However, persons over 25 years receive an adult trainee salary and have the possibility of receiving an additional employment subsidy.

---

5. Continuing education

The international evidence about the incidence of continuing education and training among young adults (16-34) is limited.[46] Table 2.2 shows how Danes fare relative to other Europeans in terms of participation in any kind of

---

46.   For Europe, one source is the EULFS *ad hoc* module on lifelong learning carried out in 2003. It contains information for the whole population of working age (15-64), with a breakdown by age group. Unfortunately, it only informs about the age group 25-34.

learning within the last 12 months: formal (being taught in the formal educational system), non-formal (being taught outside the educational system) and informal (self-learning). The participation rate in any kind of training over the 12 months preceding the survey was 82% in 2003, well above the European average of 57%.

Table 2.2. **Participation rate in any kind of learning^a by age, Denmark and Europe, 2003**

Percentages of the age group

	25-34	35-44	45-54	55-64	Total
Austria	90	88	87	93	89
Luxembourg	86	84	79	75	82
Finland	85	82	76	66	77
Denmark	**82**	**83**	**80**	**72**	**80**
Sweden	77	74	71	62	71
Slovak Republic	62	62	61	49	60
France	61	55	51	32	51
Italy	57	52	47	35	49
Portugal	54	46	39	33	44
Belgium	51	45	41	27	42
Ireland	51	52	47	42	49
Netherlands	51	44	39	30	42
Germany	50	45	41	32	42
Unite Kingdom^b	44	42	39	23	38
Poland	41	33	26	16	30
Czech Republic	34	32	28	20	29
Spain	33	26	20	14	25
Hungary	20	13	8	4	12
EU average	**57**	**53**	**49**	**40**	**51**

a) Learning activities, within the last 12 months that are not part of a formal educational programme, and are taught outside the regular educational system of schools, universities or colleges.
b) Informal training is not included.
Source: European Union Labour Force Survey (EULFS*), ad hoc* module on Lifelong Learning, 2003.

The problem is that this very encompassing definition of continuing education may include respondents that are still engaged in courses leading to an initial education qualification (known for being particularly common in Denmark). A better way of gauging participation to continuing education might be to focus on the non-formal form of training covered by the EULFS *ad hoc* survey (Table 2.3). The latter captures the learning activities that are not part of a formal educational programme, and are taught outside the regular educational system of schools, universities or colleges (but excludes self-learning via books, computers or TV programmes). This indicator confirms the previous one, as it turns out that more that more than 66% of young adults in Denmark were engaged in continuing education in 2003, which is more than the EU average of 49%.

Table 2.3.   **Participation rate in non-formal learning^a by age, Denmark and Europe, 2003**

Percentages of the age group

	25-34	35-44	45-54	55-64	Total
Luxembourg	85	83	78	75	81
Austria	85	84	84	91	86
Finland	76	74	68	60	70
Denmark	**66**	**69**	**67**	**61**	**66**
Slovak Republic	60	59	58	48	57
Sweden	57	54	53	46	53
France	54	49	46	31	46
Italy	54	50	45	35	47
Portugal	50	45	38	32	42
Ireland	46	48	44	40	45
Germany	42	40	37	30	37
Belgium	38	34	32	23	32
Netherlands	35	34	32	26	32
Poland	35	29	23	16	27
Czech Republic	24	24	21	16	21
Spain	21	17	14	9	16
Hungary	8	7	5	4	6
EU average	**49**	**47**	**44**	**38**	**45**

a)   Other learning activities within the last 12 months.

Source: European Union Labour Force Survey (EULFS), *ad hoc* module on Lifelong Learning, 2003.

In policy terms, the high incidence of continuing education in Denmark probably reflects its long tradition of investment in lifelong learning. For example, since the 19th century, Folk High Schools have been providing non-formal education, mostly in boarding schools where traditional Nordic life skills are taught.[47]

---

47   Today, there are 78 folk high schools located all around the country. The minimum age is 17½. Three folk high schools are only for young people between the ages of 16½ and 19. The courses vary in length from four days to 36 weeks. Short courses are most frequently held during the summer with participants of all

The current Danish government's objective is that everyone shall engage in lifelong learning. The Danish adult education and continuing training system indeed offers a broad variety of vocational training programmes for younger people and people with longer job experience as well as for employed and unemployed people. The year 2001 marked the introduction of a more coherent, transparent and simple structure, with education and training levels comparable to those in use in the mainstream initial education system (see Box 2.5 for more details on the range of programmes).

Box 2.5. **Training Danish workers**

The adult vocational training system serves a triple purpose:

- To contribute to maintaining and improving the vocational skills and competences of the participants in accordance with the needs on the labour market and to furthering competence development of the participants.

- To contribute to solving labour market restructuring and adaptation problems in accordance with the needs on the labour market in a short and a long term perspective.

- To give adults the possibility of upgrading competencies for the labour market as well as personal competencies through possibilities to obtain formal competencies in vocational education and training.

It comprises:

Adult vocational training programmes

This programme is largely accessible. The only entrance requirement is being resident or holding a job in Denmark. If offers mainly short vocational programmes (up to 3 000 in 2008) delivering: *i)* specific job/sector related skills and competences; *ii)* general skills and competences; and *iii)* labour management skills and competences. It also includes: *i)* special programmes for recognition of prior learning (IKV); and *ii)* specific programmes for immigrants and refugees not having adequate Danish language skills to join the ordinary adult vocational training programmes.

---

ages. The longer courses are held during the winter and the participants are normally in their early 20s. The folk high schools have a high degree of freedom to choose the subjects, content and methods of their teaching, which means that there are great differences between the schools in this respect. The subjects must be of a broad, general nature for half of the time, but the rest of the time can be spent on going into depth with special subjects and skills. General discussions about important topics are common to all the teaching.

Basic adult education programmes

The programme offers more flexible opportunities to adults who lack basic skills to attend adult vocational training courses. These comprise non-formal learning, notably work experience. The final certificate corresponds to a certificate from vocational education and training in the mainstream system at upper secondary education level.

Participants in the adult vocational training courses and/or in the basic adult education may also join or supplement the vocational training by participating in the Preparatory Adult Education, which offers courses in Danish language and mathematics for adult with low basic skills and competences.

Adult further education programmes

This consists of short-cycle tertiary education programmes for people on the labour market having a relevant educational background and at least two years of work experience.

Diploma level programmes (professional bachelor)

These are medium-cycle tertiary education programmes for people on the labour market having relevant educational background and at least two years of work experience.

Master level programmes

These are long-cycle tertiary education programmes for people on the labour market having relevant educational background and at least two years of work experience.

The study load of these last three programmes is equivalent to one year of fill-time study, but it is spread over two years so that participants may study part-time and keep their job and preserve their level of income.

Source: Information provided directly by the Danish Ministry of Employment; and Danish Ministry of Education website: *www.eng.uvm.dk/*.

The social partners play a major role in the management of this system. A National Council for Adult Vocational Education and Training advises the Minister of Education and eleven continuing training and education committees, each responsible for a specific sector of the labour market. These committees have to continuously analyse the labour market needs for new competences and develop relevant competence profiles as well as corresponding curricula. At the local level, the social partners systematically sit on the board of institutions providing adult vocational training programmes.

Adult vocational training programmes in Denmark are publicly financed to a large extent. The providers operate within a fixed financial framework largely based on the voucher principle (*i.e.* the taximeter, see Box 2.1).

There are about 120 schools licensed by the Ministry of Education to provide adult vocational training programmes all over the country. The providers are adult vocational training centres, vocational technical colleges, commercial colleges, agricultural colleges and social and health service schools. Most of the schools provide programmes for adult alongside initial education programmes attended by youth. The schools are mainly state schools, but also include a number of private schools.

There are user fees ranging from EUR 65 (DKK 500) to EUR 100 (DKK 750) per week in 2008, and representing about 15% of the operating costs. But unemployed benefit recipients usually attend for free, particularly if attendance is a requirement of an active labour market programme. Their training costs are covered by the PES (see Chapter 4 for more details). For workers, fees are usually paid by employers. What is more, workers are entitled to an allowance equivalent to the (maximum) unemployment benefit and financed by the State Grant System for Adult Training. Companies that keep paying their employees during periods of training are entitled to receiving this allowance.

6. Key points

Test scores from PISA 2003 and 2006 reveal a mixed average performance for Danish teenagers. These results should be considered in light of the country's very generous public funding of education. It amounted to 4.4% of the GDP in 2006, significantly more than the OECD average of 3.7 %. Denmark also has a relatively high drop-out rate (15-16% of its young adults do not attain upper secondary qualifications), and seems to be partially related to the failure of schools to equip disadvantaged youth with core literacy and numeracy skills.

By contrast, Denmark has a good vocational education and training (VET) system for those older than 16. VET in Denmark has a strong "dual" component, synonymous with: *i)* systematic involvement of firms and social partners and, partially as a result of that; *ii)* a high degree of job-readiness for those who complete it.

More on the negative side, Denmark has among the oldest students and graduates in OECD countries. Unless Danes effectively retire later,[48] this means less active years spent in the labour market by educated individuals. In the Welfare Agreement approved in 2006, a number of measures were

---

48   The employment rate of workers aged 55-64 in 2008 was well above the corresponding rate in OECD and in the European Union (respectively, 58%, 54% and 47%).

announced to cope with this problem. The single most important change for a student will consist of making access to tertiary education easier if less than two years have elapsed between schooling completion and tertiary education enrolment. As to the providers, new "financing structures will bring actual study times better in line with scheduled study times".

Finally, it is worth stressing the country's high incidence of continuing/lifelong education. Denmark offers a broad variety of training programmes as well as much financial support to its citizens (unemployed or not) and its firms are willing to invest in lifelong learning.

CHAPTER 3

DEMAND-SIDE OPPORTUNITIES AND BARRIERS

Although education and training policies are central elements of any long-term effective strategy for improving youth labour market prospects, a comprehensive policy framework has to pay attention to opportunities and constraints on the labour market. It must pay particular attention to the labour market arrangements and institutions and their impact on the demand for young people, specifically those with no or limited education or lacking labour market experience.

Section 1 examines the current economic situation and employment opportunities in general in Denmark. Section 2 explores the macro-economic determinants of youth unemployment, its sensitivity to the business cycle, in particular how it is impacted by the current economic recession. The following sections examine wages and labour market institutions. Section 3 looks at the relative wages of young people and Section 4 reviews labour contract regulation that could affect the entry of youth into the labour market. Finally, Section 5 reviews the evidence on wage gaps between young women and young men.

1. GDP growth and overall employment in Denmark

A.   *Until recently*

Up to 2006, the Danish economy enjoyed sustained growth and tight labour markets, and between 2004 and 2006, the annual GDP growth was between 2.3 and 3.3% (Figures 3.1 and 3.2). In 2007, the economy grew by only 1.6% but this modest performance apparently reflected capacity constraints, including major labour shortages. Capacity utilisation rose close to historical peaks and skilled labour shortages – partially due to a quasi-stagnant labour supply (Figure 3.3) – became a more prominent constraint holding back production. The annual GDP growth turned negative (-1.2%) in 2008 but the overall unemployment rate remained very low, around 3%.

Figure 3.1.   **GDP growth, Denmark *versus* Germany, Sweden and the United States, 1991-2008**

Gross domestic product, constant 2000 prices, annual percentage change

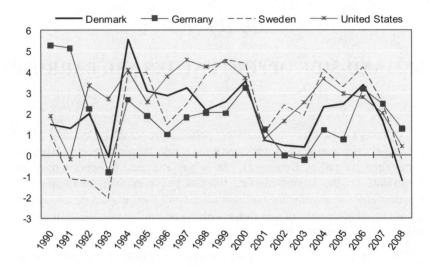

Source: OECD National Accounts database.

Part of the need for extra workers was met by an increase in foreign labour inflows. Strong labour demand in the Danish economy translated into an influx of temporary migrants[49] and a rise in the number of cross-border commuters coming from Germany or Sweden. Particularly the construction and manufacturing sectors benefited from this additional labour force.

Yet, at that stage of the business cycle, opening doors and cutting paperwork was enough to combat a structural deficit of skills. Figures from the Danish Economic Council (2007a) show that 20% of foreign workers leave within a year and 40% of them within two years, partially as a consequence of the country's restrictive work permits policy. A related issue is the role of the country's high marginal taxation rates in discouraging high-skilled immigration.

---

49.   As a result of the EU enlargement, Denmark has decided to establish a transitory period (2004-09) for free movement of citizens from Estonia, Latvia, Lithuania, Poland, the Slovak Republic, Slovenia, the Czech Republic and Hungary. During this period, workers need to apply for a work and residence permit to become eligible for working in Denmark.

Figure 3.2.   **Total unemployment rate, Denmark, Germany, Sweden and the United States, 1990-2008**

Percentages of the labour force

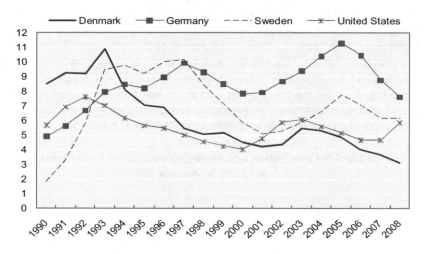

Source: OECD Labour Force database.

Figure 3.3.   **Total civilian employment and total labour force, Denmark, Germany, Sweden and the United States, 1995-2008**

1995=100

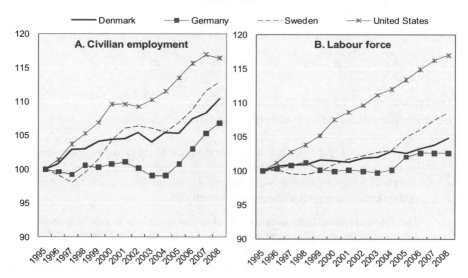

Source: OECD Labour Force database.

B.   Recent developments

In the immediate future, issues of concern to Danish policy makers will include rising unemployment. The world is indeed facing a severe economic crisis that is affecting Denmark and is currently deteriorating the labour market prospects of many of its citizens. Danish unemployment statistics up to September 2009 show a rapid deterioration of the situation (Figure 3.4), particularly for youth.[50] The unemployment rate of youth aged 16-24 has more than doubled in September 2009 since January 2008, while that of young adults (aged 25-29) has risen by 80%, more in line with the evolution of the overall unemployment rate.[51] A reassuring element, however, is that this surge intervened when youth unemployment rate reached an historical low.

Figure 3.4.   **Industrial production and unemployment rate,[a] by age group, Denmark, January 2008-September 2009**

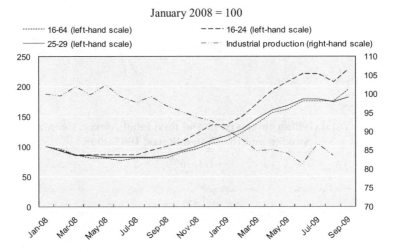

January 2008 = 100

a)   Unemployed registered at the PES (seasonally adjusted).

Source: Statistics Denmark and *OECD Main Economic Indicators database*.

50.   Data used in Figure 3.4 are administrative data which differ from labour force survey data. A difference regarding youth is that a student who declares in the survey that he wants a job is counted in the labour force while he is not included in the Danish administrative unemployment data.

51.   The unemployment rate index highlighted here and in Figure 3.4 should not be confused with unemployment rate levels. For instance, in September 2009, among the three age groups considered here, the 16-24-year-olds had the lowest unemployment rate, and the 25-29-year-olds was the group with the highest unemployment rate.

2. Youth unemployment and the business cycle

This recent increase of the youth unemployment rate in Denmark echoes similar developments taking place in other OECD countries. And they replicate to a large extent labour market patterns observed in the past during economic recessions.

Using time series date covering the past four decades, it is indeed relatively easy to show that for the OECD on average, each one negative percentage point deviation from the GDP's long-term growth rate leads to 0.65 percentage point increase of the adult (25-54) unemployment rate. But the equivalent youth (15-24) unemployment rate increment is 1.36 percentage point (Table 3.1, Col. 2).

Results for Denmark point at slightly higher reactivity for adult workers (Table 3.1). A one negative percentage point deviation from the GDP's long-term growth rate usually translates into a 0.92 percentage point increase of the adult unemployment rate. And the Danish youth (15-24) unemployment rate usually rises by 1.1 percentage points. This is more than the adult reactivity, but less than elsewhere in the OECD in similar circumstances.

Table 3.1.   **How the unemployment rate responds to 1 percentage point (negative) deviation of the GDP growth rate,[a] Denmark *versus* all OECD countries**

	Denmark	OECD (all countries pooled)
Youth (15-24)	1.10	1.36
Adults (25-54)	0.92	0.66
Senior (55-64)	0.64	0.45

a) A crucial input of the analysis is the GDP data. Annual GDP time series consist of GDP chained linked volume index, with base year 2000. We are particularly interested in the consequences of GDP shocks, where the term "shocks" refer to deviations from the long run trend. To capture these shocks we resort to de-trending techniques. Our GDP data are de trended with a Hodrick Prescott (1997) filter. This methodology basically consists in minimising a function of the sum of the cyclical part of a time-series plus the sum of the squares of the trend component's second differences, multiplied by a given parameter λ. Following a large literature and given the annual frequency of the data, a parameter $\lambda = 6.25$ was chosen.

Source: OECD Labour Force database for unemployment rates and *OECD Annual National Accounts database* for GDP.

Examination of how youth and adult unemployment rates are related conveys the same message (Figure 3.5). Youth (15-24) and adult (25-64) unemployment rates are highly correlated in Denmark. Youth unemployment rates vary in response to variations in economic conditions as do adult unemployment rates, increasing in recessions and recovering during periods of expansion.

Figure 3.5.   **Youth[a] and adult[b] unemployment rates, Denmark, 1983-2007**

Percentages

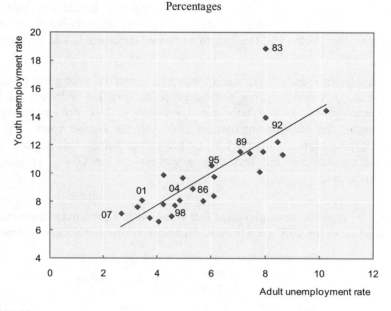

a)   Aged 15-24.
b)   Aged 25-54.
Source: OECD Labour Force database.

The estimated slope of the linear trend on display in Figure 3.5 is about 1.14, meaning that a 1 percentage point increase (decrease) of the adult unemployment rate translates into a 1.14 percentage point increment (reduction) of the youth unemployment rate. This youth *versus* adult pattern based on historical data is thus remarkably similar to the very recent developments on display on Figure 3.4.

Conventionally, labour economists expect youth unemployment rates to be higher and more sensitive than adult unemployment rates to changes in aggregate demand for labour. Here are some of the main reasons.

First, much research has shown that the first reaction of firms in a downturn is to cease hiring before commencing on the more expensive procedure of redundancies. It is evident that young people comprise a disproportionate segment of job seekers and thus are more heavily affected by a recruitment freeze.

Second, for employers, the cost of firing young people is generally lower than for older workers. Having less experience than the long-term insiders, they embody lower levels of investment by firms in specific training and consequently involve a smaller loss to firms making them redundant. Moreover, young people are more likely to be subject to the LIFO (last-in first-out) rule. Almost invariably, employment protection legislation (EPL) requires a qualifying period before it can be invoked and typically compensation for redundancy increases with tenure/seniority. Thus, also for these reasons, the more recently hired employees will be cheaper to fire. Obviously, this will disproportionately affect young people (O'Higgins, 1997). However, it is worth stressing that in Denmark the EPL asymmetry between young and older workers is nil or at least very limited compared with other OECD countries (more on this in Section 4).[52] Other things being equal, it implies that the overall cost of the economic crisis in terms of job destructions should be less concentrated on young workers.

Third, young people are more likely to voluntarily quit their jobs than older workers.[53] If such voluntary quitting or behaviour or "shopping around" is less cyclically sensitive than job availability, one consequence is that when job opportunities become scarce, unemployment will increase more amongst those groups with a higher likelihood of quitting their jobs (Moser, 1986).

---

52.   For example Spain, Poland or France.

53.   Their initial experiences in the labour market are likely to involve a certain amount of "shopping around" in so far as circumstances permit, so as to find an appropriate occupation. The opportunity cost of doing so is lower for young people. They will tend to have less experience and lower wages, and are less likely to "need" a job to support a family. Blanchflower and Freeman (1996) report that, in the United States, young people between the ages of 16 and 25 typically hold 7-8 different jobs.

3. Starting wages and labour relations

A.   *No legal minimum wage but relatively high starting wages for low educated workers*

There is no statutory national minimum wage in Denmark. For those covered by collective agreements, hiring wages are regulated by trade agreements resulting from the collective bargaining between the social partners. They reflect a host of factors, like previous work experience, the nature of the work, whether it is day-time work or evening work etc. Age is only a determining factor under the age of 18 and with respect to apprenticeship (see Chapter 2, Section 4).

In 2007, about one-out-two workers of the private sector was part of a collective agreement with an explicit wage floor. The agreed minimum wage varies from sector to sector with the lowest in 2007 being around EUR 12 (DKK 90) per hour, but with many agreements having a minimum wage of around EUR 13 (DKK 100) per hour.

B.   *Wage profiles*

In the absence of statutory minimum wage, it makes sense to focus on actual wages and benefits received by workers. European data (EUSILC) can be used to compute relative age-wage profiles that can be compared internationally (Figure 3.6).

The usual pattern emerges: younger people earn less than older ones. In 2007, relative earnings profiles in Denmark were very similar to those observed on average across the European Union, except perhaps for prime-age individuals holding tertiary education qualifications (>ISCED 3) for whom relative pay appears much inferior to what it is on average in Europe. This confirms that the tertiary graduate gross wage premium is quite low in Denmark by OECD standards (see Figure 2.10 for more evidence on this), and in line with the "compressed wage structure" story often referred to in Nordic countries.

Figure 3.6.   **Wage profiles of full-time workers, by educational attainment, Denmark and Europe,[a] 2007**

Percentages of average monthly gross wage among 15-64-year-olds, all educational levels pooled

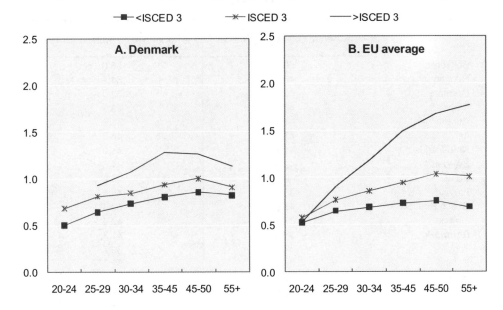

a)   Unweighted average of Austria, Belgium, Czech Republic, Denmark, Finland, France, Germany, Greece, Hungary, Iceland, Ireland, Italy, Luxembourg, Netherlands, Norway, Poland, Portugal, Slovak Republic, Spain, Sweden and the United Kingdom.

Source: European Survey on Income and Living Conditions (EUSILC).

4. Non-wage costs and other barriers to employment

A.   *Non-wage costs*

The tax-wedge – the difference between what employers pay out in wages and social security charges and what employees take home after tax social security deductions and cash benefits – has also to be taken into account. Table 3.2 (3rd column) indicates that Denmark's tax wedge in 2008 was intermediate compared to those registered in other OECD countries. This result also holds for low-wage earners (2nd column). In fact, indirect wage costs (*i.e.* social security contributions) are very low in Denmark by international standards, whilst the rate of direct taxation of wage income is high (Westergaard-Nielsen, 2006).

Table 3.2.　　**Tax wedge including employer social security contributions in OECD countries, 2008**

Percentages

	Tax wedge on low-wage earner[a]	Tax wedge on average earner[b]
Belgium	50.3	56.0
Hungary	46.7	54.1
Germany	47.3	52.0
France	45.5	49.3
Austria	44.4	48.8
Italy	43.0	46.5
Netherlands	41.7	45.0
Sweden	42.5	44.6
EU19	**39.8**	**43.9**
Finland	38.3	43.5
Czech Republic	40.0	43.4
Greece	37.6	42.4
Denmark	**38.9**	**41.2**
Turkey	37.6	39.7
Poland	38.7	39.7
Slovak Republic	36.1	38.9
Spain	33.8	37.8
Norway	34.3	37.7
Portugal	32.9	37.6
OECD	**33.5**	**37.4**
Luxembourg	29.6	35.9
United Kingdom	29.7	32.8
Canada	26.6	31.3
United States	28.0	30.1
Japan	28.0	29.5
Switzerland	26.5	29.5
Iceland	23.7	28.3
Australia	21.9	26.9
Ireland	16.0	22.9
New Zealand	18.2	21.2
Korea	17.4	20.3
Mexico	10.9	15.1

Countries are ranked by descending tax wedge on low-wage earner.

a)　Total tax wedge including employer mandatory social security contributions for a single worker with no children earning 67% of the average production wage.

b)　Total tax wedge including employer mandatory social security contributions for a single worker with no children earning the average production wage.

Source: OECD Taxing Wages database.

B.   *Employment protection and dismissal rules*

Theoretically, very strict employment protection could negatively affect employment prospects for low-skilled and inexperienced workers, by restraining employers' willingness to take a risk on them. But the OECD indicator of the strictness of employment protection at 1.91 in 2008 (Figure 3.7) suggests that Denmark has one of the less strict employment legislation frameworks in Europe. This probably reflects the Danish internationally praised "flexicurity" model (see Box 3.1 for more details) where generous unemployment and welfare benefits are granted in exchange for very little legal job protection (Westergaard-Nielsen, 2006).

Figure 3.7.   **Overall strictness of employment protection and its three main components, 2008**[a]

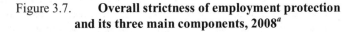

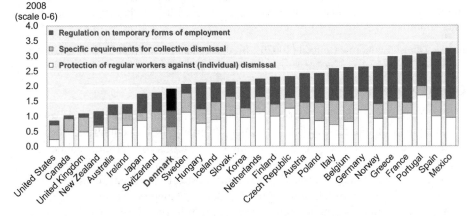

a)   Countries are ranked from left to right in ascending order of the overall summary index.

Source: OECD Employment Protection database.

Box 3.1. **Flexicurity**

Flexicurity – the contraction of the English words, flexibility and security – is currently a popular concept for employment and labour market reforms in many OECD countries. In recent years, Denmark has become the prime example of a real-life flexicurity labour market. The Danish case of flexicurity is a combination a flexible labour market with liberal hiring-and firing procedures on the one hand, and relatively generous social security and active labour market policies on the other hand. In general terms, Denmark has succeeded in combining: *i)* relative generous unemployment benefit schemes; *ii)* an active labour market policy and *iii)* flexible employment contracts. The first two ingredients are covered extensively in Chapter 4). The focus hereafter in on the third one.

There are a couple of numerical indicators that suggest that Danish workers change jobs more often than elsewhere. Denmark is among a group of countries with a rather low average tenure with the same employer (around 8.5 years in 2005). In contrast, the average tenure of 12 years in Japan in year 2000 is almost 50% higher than in Denmark. The average number of jobs held per worker in Denmark is also the highest in Europe; almost six jobs in Denmark, compared to four jobs on average in EU-25. More than 70% of people in Denmark think that changing jobs every few years is good, compared with 40% in Europe.

The high degree of mobility from employer to employer is probably linked to the relatively modest level of job protection. Low job protection exists since the 1980s and is consistent with the Danish industrial structure dominated by small and medium-sized enterprises. In practice, almost all Danish workers should be considered as "temporary" workers who can be dismissed upon short notice. Such flexibility is also attributable to the tradition whereby the social partners regulate most of the terms and conditions important to the labour market themselves, as opposed to the state regulation found in other countries.

Source: Danish Economic Council (2007b); Bredgaard and Larsen (2007), OECD (2004b).

5. Gender wage gap

There may also be barriers to employment and equal pay for some categories of workers, typically women. In many OECD countries, despite dramatic educational gains by women[54] in terms of tertiary education participation and completion, women are behind in terms of labour market outcomes. How does Denmark fare in this respect? A recent release of the *OECD Employment Outlook* (OECD, 2008c, Chapter 3) shows that in Denmark women's employment gap in relation to men is about 8.8%,[55] one of the lowest across the OECD.

There is few available international evidence about gender wage gap. But one can again turn to the EUSILC survey to get some evidence on this important labour market outcome. Using the gross monthly earnings information of young workers aged 16-29 it contains, one can estimate a series of log-linear earnings[56] equations that include a gender dummy.

---

54. In Australia, for example, young women have higher educational attainment than young men. By the age of 24, 80% of women had completed upper secondary education in 2007 compared with 71% for men (OECD, 2009b).

55. The gender employment gap is defined as the difference between male and female employment rates as a percentage of the male employment rate.

56. The advantage of the log-linear specification of the wage W is that it generates estimates for the X explanatory variable coefficient that are easy to interpret as

Table 3.3 reports the results for a model that just control for age, education and labour supply[57] of the respondents. They confirm the existence of a gross (monthly) wage gap between men and women of equal age, equal educational attainment[58] and who are similar in terms of supply of labour. The average of coefficients points at an unaccounted gap of 20% across Europe, whereas the estimated unaccounted gap for Denmark is above at 25%. This high gap compares unfavourably with that of the Netherlands, Ireland, the United Kingdom or Germany, where it is virtually non-existent.

Danish research allows going one step further in explaining the gender wage gap. Analysing wage data covering the period 1997-2006, Deding and Larsen (2008) find that 70 to 80% of the gross wage gap[59] can be explained by gender differences in terms of work experience, occupation/position within firms or the chosen sector or industry.

The gender-biased allocation across sectors or industry pointed out by Deding and Larsen (2008) could be partially attributed to systematic difference in terms of fields of study within a certain educational group,[60] leading to a gender-biased allocation across sectors or industries. There is indeed international evidence of a persistent bias gap as to the type of tertiary education[61] (> ISCED 3) chosen by young women resulting in occupation segregation.[62] Women still dominate within teacher training, pedagogy, health and social care, whereas men dominate within the natural sciences, engineering or advanced VET programmes (OECD, 2008b).

---

they correspond to points of percentage of change of the wage level. For a model $log\ W = \beta 0 + \beta 1X + \varepsilon$ there is indeed that $\beta 1 = dlnW/dX = (dW/W)/dX \approx (WX+1 - WX)/WX$ when $dX=1$.

57.   Average number of hours of work per week.

58.   Using ISCED categories.

59.   Ranging from 17 to 21%.

60.   All individuals with a tertiary educational attainment for instance.

61.   This issue should not be confused with that of the overall propensity of women *versus* men to participate in tertiary education. It is well establish that in many OECD countries, including Denmark, young women now outnumber their male counterparts in tertiary education completion.

62.   Canadian female graduates, for instance, are overrepresented in low-paid fields (arts and humanities, education) and underrepresented in those that offer higher earnings prospects (engineering, computer sciences) (OECD, 2008b).

Table 3.3.　　**Female wage gap, young women aged 16-29, Europe, 2007**

OLS coefficients (and p-value in italics)[a]

	Estimate	P values
Spain	-0.28	0.0000
Norway	-0.27	0.0002
Denmark	**-0.25**	**0.0000**
Poland	-0.25	0.0000
Iceland	-0.23	0.0002
Austria	-0.23	0.0000
Greece	-0.22	0.0000
Portugal	-0.22	0.0000
Sweden	-0.22	0.0006
Finland	-0.21	0.0001
Slovak Rep.	-0.20	0.0000
Belgium	-0.20	0.0000
Czech Rep.	-0.18	0.0000
Italy	-0.16	0.0000
Luxembourg	-0.15	0.0008
Hungary	-0.12	0.0007
France	-0.11	0.0050
United Kingdom	-0.07	0.0112
Germany	-0.02	0.6980
Ireland	0.01	0.7738
Netherlands	0.03	0.4196
EU unweighted average	-0.17	

a)   Estimated model is log- linear. List of controls includes: highest educational attainment (ISCED 1 to 6), age, age square, and hours worked per week. The gender gap is captured by a gender dummy variable (1=Women, 0=Men).

Source: European Survey on Income and Living Conditions (EUSILC).

6. Key points

Until very recently Denmark was characterised by tight labour markets. Capacity utilisation rose close to historical peaks and skilled labour shortages became a more prominent constraint. A tight market also implied better labour market opportunities for low-educated youth or young immigrants.

However, in the immediate future, issues of concern to Danish policy makers will include rising youth unemployment. The world is indeed facing a global economic crisis that is affecting Denmark and is currently deteriorating the labour market prospects of many Danish citizens.

This said, Denmark's labour market institutions are supposedly conducive to good employment prospects for youth, and this should help quickly reduce youth unemployment, when, hopefully the economy starts picking up. Other elements should encourage risk-averse employers to recruit inexperienced youth with longer-than-usual unemployment spells. They comprise: *i)* a moderate tax-wedge by European standards; and, what is more *ii)* a relatively lax employment protection framework.

CHAPTER 4

THE ROLE OF WELFARE
AND ACTIVATION POLICIES

Under normal economic circumstances, active labour market programmes (ALMPs), such as job-search assistance, training and employment incentive schemes, play an important role during the school-to-work transition period for youth, especially for the low-skilled ones. During an economic recession that significantly reduces job opportunities for the labour-market entrants, an adequate safety net in combination with well-designed ALMPs is important to preventing youth poverty, disengagement from the labour market and human capital depreciation. Effective ALMPs can also contribute to rapid (re)integration into employment, once the economic growth picks up again.

This chapter outlines recent developments in passive (Section 1) and active (Section 3) labour market programmes for youth in Denmark, while focusing on its renowned youth activation strategy introduced in the mid-1990s (Section 2). Finally, the chapter briefly reviews the role of Public Employment Services (PES) (Section 4).

1. The role of passive labour market measures

Unemployed youth in Denmark are covered by one of the most generous income-support schemes in the OECD area, either in the form of unemployment insurance benefits or in the form of social assistance benefits (cash benefits).

A.   *Unemployment insurance benefits (UIB)*

UIB are available to school-leavers without work experience

In Denmark, only members of unemployment insurance funds can receive UIB and membership is voluntary. Benefit eligibility is in general conditional on a minimum of 52 weeks employment history in non-subsidised jobs within the past three years (a minimum of 34 weeks during the past three years for part-time employment). However, school-leavers with no employment history can also receive UIB as soon as they start looking for work conditional on two conditions being met: *i)* school-leavers must have completed a "qualifying education" lasting a minimum of 18 months;[63] and *ii)* they have to join an unemployment insurance fund no later than two weeks after completing school.

The unemployment insurance system in Denmark, which covers both employees and self-employed persons aged 18 to 64, is managed by funds which are usually associations of employees and/or the self-employed and are closely related to trade unions (OECD, 2005a). They are funded by membership fees and, to a smaller degree, contributions from employers who lay off members of unemployment insurance funds. But unemployment insurance funds are also highly (2/3) subsidised by the state, in a clearly countercyclical way. Membership fees did not changed substantially during the past decade. It is the state subsidy that varied with the level of unemployment. Therefore tax payers bear the full increase in the costs of financing benefits when the level of unemployment rises. This means that labour unions and employer organisations risk not fully taking into account the costs of unemployment to society (Danish Economic Council, 2002).

At a more micro level, the Danish unemployment insurance system embodies welfare principles rather than insurance principles, judging by the main features of the system, such as the low upper ceilings combined with high net replacement rates and uniform maximum benefit duration regardless of contribution history (Leschke, 2007).

Meanwhile, unemployment insurance is becoming less popular among youth. In 2008, the memberships rate was more than 80% among Danish workers aged 30-49, but only 16% among young workers aged under 25, down from 24% in 2001 (Figure 4.1). According to a study carried out by the Association of Unemployment Insurance Funds in September 2006, few youth in Denmark today are knowledgeable about the nature of an unemployment insurance fund (Jørgensen, 2006). They confuse unemployment insurance funds with trade unions or with the social assistance system delivered by municipalities.

---

63. The underlying logic is that the applicant must have: *i)* completed 18-month-long upper secondary education (ISCED 3); and *ii)* acquired qualifications that are relevant for the specific unemployment insurance fund he/she is joining.

Figure 4.1.   **Membership of unemployment insurance funds, by age group, Denmark, 2001-08**

Percentages of workers by age group

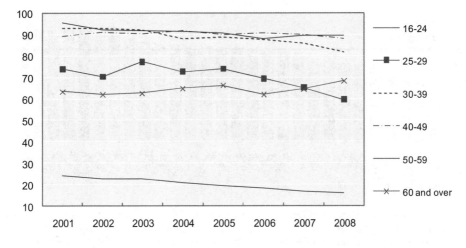

Source: StatBank Denmark.

But school-leavers receive lower unemployment insurance benefits (UIB) than those with an employment record

School-leavers without regular work experience receive lower UIB. While members with adequate work experience can receive up to 90% of their former salary or a given maximum, inexperienced school-leavers receive a flat rate amounting to 82% of that maximum.64 However, many youth rapidly accumulate sufficient labour experience to qualify for the standard replacement regime, mainly because they held student jobs while studying.

Granting a high gross replacement rate, the Danish unemployment insurance benefit system is considered to be among the more generous among OECD countries. International comparisons of UIB net replacement rates[65] faced by single persons without children with a low wage show that the net replacement rate in Denmark for a low-paid worker is close to 75% and is above the OECD average (Figure 4.2).

64.   In 2009, the maximum weekly unemployment insurance benefit was EUR 487 (DKK 3 625) and EUR 400 (DKK 2 975) per week for school-leavers.

65.   The net replacement rate is an indicator that compares income from work to benefit income and is adjusted for the effects of taxation.

Figure 4.2.   **Net unemployment benefit^a replacement rates, OECD countries, 2006**

Percentages

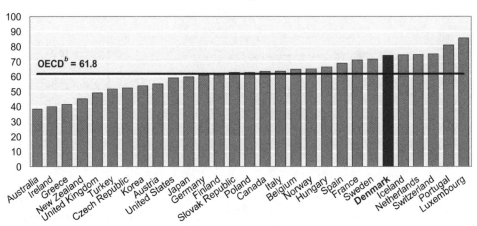

a)   These data are net replacement rates, *i.e.* they are adjusted for the effects of taxation. They refer to an average of net replacement rates faced by single persons without children with pre-unemployment earnings of 67% and 100% of the average wage. They relate to the initial phase of unemployment after any waiting period. No social assistance "top-ups" are assumed to be available in either the in-work or out-of-work situation. Any income taxes payable on UIB are determined in relation to annualised benefit values even if the maximum benefit duration is shorter than 12 months.

b)   Unweighted average.

Source: OECD Tax-Benefit Models, *www.oecd.org/els/social/workincentives.*

The duration of unemployment insurance receipt is long but strictly conditional

Unemployed Danes can collect UIB during at most four years within a six-year period. This is a long duration by international standard, even it is much shorter than in the early 1990s where it was nine years. However, UIB recipients have strict obligations to follow. As a rule, every UIB recipient should be registered as unemployed at the local PES and should actively search for a job. He/she has to apply for all jobs which he/she can manage and must be able to start a job with one day's notice. All unemployed people will, after some time, receive an individual action plan organising regular mandatory contacts with the PES as well as participate in ALMPs. In general, recipients must accept various offers of activation programmes after nine months. Rules are however stricter for youth, and particularly for low-educated youth (more on this in Section 2 below).

B.   Social assistance

Social assistance is available to deprived or uninsured youth

In parallel with the unemployment insurance system, there is a social assistance scheme in Denmark implemented under the joint responsibility of the Ministry of Interior and Social Affairs and the 98 municipalities. It is delivered by the latter. The unemployed who are not members of an unemployment insurance fund or those who face UIB termination can apply for social assistance, which basically consists of cash benefits. Youth under 25 years receiving social assistance benefits resuming education should apply for an education grant. If they refuse to go back to education, they cannot get any benefits.

Social assistance benefits are means-tested and available to any adults who are unable because of particular circumstances (sickness, unemployment) temporarily, for a shorter or longer period, to provide for themselves either through work, support from their spouse or through other social services (Jespersen *et al.*, 2008). There are no conditions relating to age in terms of access. In practice, however, social assistance is seldom given to children under 18 because they are presumably supported by their parents. If an individual chooses not to join an unemployment insurance fund and becomes unemployed, he/she is eligible for social assistance.

Recent reforms ensure that social assistance benefits are lower than the unemployment insurance benefits (UIBs). The starting level is 80% of the maximum UIB for parents with children living in Denmark (60% of the maximum of UIB for persons with no children) and the benefits are reduced after six months to the level of an education grant.

Municipal authorities have to offer activation measures to people receiving social assistance. Beneficiaries with no other problem than unemployment must actively look for a job. Such an offer will normally last for a continuous period of at least four weeks. Payment is suspended if the beneficiary refuses without reason to participate in an activation measure or repeatedly refuse a job opportunity (see following section for more details on activation measures).

C.   Only a very small group of youth receive UIB or social assistance

The number of unemployed youth receiving UIB has declined since 2003 (Figure 4.3), in line with the overall reduction in youth unemployment (Figure 4.5). In 2008, 0.2% of the age group 16-24 and 1.2% of the age group 25-24 received UIB while the corresponding proportions were 0.5%

and 0.6% for social assistance benefits. Youth aged less than 25 receive in general more often social assistance benefits than UIB, while it is the opposite for older youth.

Figure 4.3.   **Unemployed youth by type of benefit^a and age group, 2000-08**

Percentages of population by age group

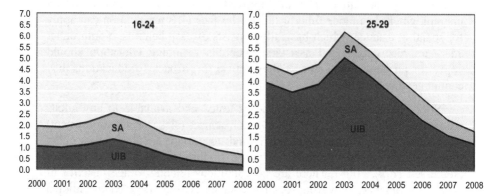

SA: social assistance; UIB: unemployment insurance benefit.

a)   Data refer to monthly figures in December each year.

Source: StatBank Denmark, *www.statbank.dk/AUAAR01.*

D.   *Sickness and disability benefits*

An issue worth keeping in sight is the rise in the number of youth (15-29) receiving disability benefits in Denmark (Figure 4.4). Such a trend is found in other OECD countries (OECD, 2008d), especially the Netherlands and Norway (OECD, 2008a, d). Although the at-risk population remains clearly biased against older age groups,[66] recent years have seen a large increase in the inflow into disability benefits by young people. This is at odds with the generally high health premium associated with being young.

---

66.   In 2008, youth aged 15-29 represented 10% of new recipients of disability benefits.

Figure 4.4.   **Trend in new disability benefit recipients, youth[a] and adults,[b] Denmark, 1998-2008**

1998=100

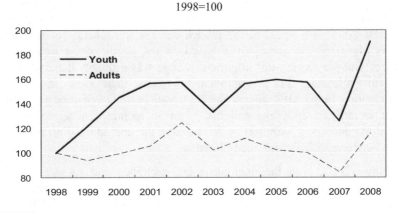

a) Aged 15-29.
b) Aged 30-66.
Source: National Social Appeals Board.

The most worrying element is that entering health-related benefits at a young age may act as a long-term inactivity trap. The international evidence about rehabilitation programmes is that they seem to be relatively ineffective at assisting benefit recipients back into employment – at least as they currently operate (OECD, 2009c) This tentatively means that Denmark's activation challenge towards youth not only consists of reducing the number of unemployed but also bringing down the caseload of those young persons who end up being considered as "disabled", presumably after a long period on sick leave.

2. The role of activation

A.   *Activation policies for the unemployed*

A sequence of reforms initiated in the mid-1990s, and fine-tuned since, has radically shifted the system from a passive focus on income maintenance to a more active emphasis on bringing unemployed into employment. The main ingredients of the policy changes introduced since the mid-1990s comprise: *i)* a shortening of the benefit duration; *ii)* the abolition of the possibility to re-gained UIB eligibility *via* participation in activation measures; and *iii)* the introduction of activation requirements both in the unemployment insurance scheme and in the social assistance scheme.

The 1994 labour market reform was key in the implementation of this agenda (Danish Economic Council, 2002 and 2007a). The reform marked the adoption of a strong "mutual obligations" culture. After nine months of unemployment benefit, eligibility should be conditional on participation in ALMPs. Another element of the reform was the introduction of individual action plans for the unemployed based on the needs of the local labour market. But the single most important change was probably the abolition of the rule allowing the unemployed to renew their right to UIB by participating in ALMPs. Since, the right can be only regained by regular work for at least 26 weeks within the last 36 months. These moves were aimed at combating "carousel" effects where the unemployed go back-and-forth between ALMPs and unemployment.

Since 2003, both the unemployment insurance and social assistance systems implement similar activation routines. For instance, all unemployed individuals regardless of their benefit status are referred to the PES for ALMP delivery (Kluve *et al.*, 2007; see Section 4 on the Public Employment Service). From the summer of 2009, implementation of ALMPs will be solely the responsibility of municipalities.

B.   *Activation policies for unemployed youth*

Youth activation, a central feature in Denmark

While, by the mid-1990s, activation became a central feature of the Danish labour market, its implementation was gradually improved and intensified, especially in relation to youth.

Denmark's first compulsory youth activation programme, the Youth Allowance Programme (YAP), directed towards social assistance claimants (uninsured unemployed) aged 18-19 was introduced in 1990. Since then, the activation scheme has been gradually extended to cover all youth aged less than 30 benefiting from social assistance. Until the summer of 2009, they must take part in activation programmes and receive reduced benefits equivalent to education grants after a maximum of three months (*versus* nine months for older individuals) of unemployment. Refusal to participate entails the loss of benefits.

In 1996, the YAP was supplemented by the Youth Unemployment Programme (YUP), targeted at the insured unemployed aged 18-25. Since YUP's inception, low-educated youth (without upper secondary education or ISCED 3), who have been receiving UIB for six months during the past nine months, are obliged to participate in 18-months long training programmes. But the single most important measure was the decision to halve UIB after six months of unemployment. This reduction also results in eliminating the gap between unemployment benefits and education grants, thus serving as an incentive for the young unemployed to undertake ordinary education on education grants or to find a job (Jensen *et al.*, 2003). Refusal to participate in the special education programmes or to enter the ordinary education system is followed by a sanction, going in theory as far as a total loss of benefits. In 1999 these elements was extended to include better educated youth aged less than 25 as well.

Strengthening activation for all young unemployment-insured adult, even single parents?

Proposals have been made in Denmark to extend the tighter benefit rules (*i.e.* the 50% cut after six months of unemployment) applicable to youth aged less than 25 so that they also cover youth aged 25-29. This recommendation was included in the final report of the Welfare Commission in 2006, as well as the recommendation to shorten the duration of UIB for youth from four to two and a half years. But the 2006 Welfare Reform agreed upon by a parliamentary majority did not follow these recommendations. Older youth still receive higher UIB than their younger peers and the maximum UIB duration remained unchanged at four years (Danish Economic Council, 2007b).

The Labour Market Commission established in 2007 to provide recommendations on how to achieve the employment goals required by the government's 2015 Plan for fiscal policy released its final report in August 2009 (OECD, 2009f). The Labour Market Commission recommends that the arrangement whereby unemployed people under 25 receive reduced UIB rates should be extended to unemployed people between 25 and 29 without children. However, leaving single young parents aside of any compulsory activation towards education or employment could be questioned.

C.   Youth activation in practice in 2009

General activation rules

In Denmark, all newly unemployed, irrespective of their age, are required to immediately register with a local PES (called a job centre). Within a month they must post their curriculum vitae (CV) on *Jobnet*[67] and

---

67.   Jobnet is the public Job Centre Internet facility for all job seekers and employers in Denmark. It contains most job offers and CVs in Denmark, and has more than two million visitors every month. At Jobnet, job seekers can also find information on job searching, training and recruiting of new employees (*www.jobnet.dk*). In

subsequently update it on a weekly basis. The PES must promptly assess of the job seeker's employability using job-profiling software in combination with in-depth interviews by caseworkers in order to quickly identify those who are at risk of ending up in long-term unemployment.

The unemployed must document that he or she is actively seeking for work and should apply for at least four jobs per week. After one month, there is a mandatory meeting with the unemployment insurance fund. The unemployed person then has to contact the PES and the unemployment insurance fund every three months in order to receive job search counselling and to be checked his/her availability for work (European Employment Observatory, 2008).

Currently, any "reasonable" job must be accepted from the first day of unemployment, regardless of previous occupation of the unemployed. This means the acceptance of up to four hours of commuting each day, although the implementation of this rule may not be very strict (Dingeldey, 2007). Recipients who do not comply (for instance miss a appointment with their caseworker or refuse to participate in a programme) face sanctions. In most cases (80% of all cases), individuals lose a couple days' worth of unemployment benefits. In very rare cases, individuals can lose benefit entitlements for several weeks or more (Geerdsen and Holm, 2007).

Different activation rules according to age, educational attainment and family obligations

Activation rules are the same for recipients of social assistance or UIB. However, the time limit within which an individual action plan is drawn up and the unemployed person is ascribed to an ALMP and the type of active measures – *i.e.* the maximal duration of the "passive" period – varies between age groups, educational attainment and family situation (Table 4.1). Benefit recipients aged less than 30 have to participate in activation measures within three months of unemployment. If they lack an upper secondary educational attainment, the activation measure must be related to education and preferably, ordinary education. However, for young parents aged less than 25 as well as for benefit recipients aged 25-30, return to ordinary education is not mandatory. By contrast, any activation measure starts after nine months for benefit recipients aged 30-60 years or more (and after six months for those older than 60). It should be noted that these time limits are minimum requirements; many job centres propose ALMPs at a much earlier stage (Kluve *et al.*, 2007).

2009, the website Jobnet has been given extra resources to provide a better overview of internships and student jobs.

Table 4.1.   **Activation process by age, educational level and family situation, from 1ˢᵗ August 2009, Denmark**

Age under 30

General rule: Have to be activated before 13 weeks of continuous unemployment for a period of six months. All active measures can be used to activate recipients

Rules for special groups of youth

Under 25 without upper secondary education	Without children	*Not ready to enrol in an educational programme* Activation towards making recipients ready for ordinary education
		Ready to enrol in an educational programme Activation towards compulsory enrolment in ordinary education
	With children	Enrolling in an educational programme at the upper secondary level is not an obligation but is possible
Unemployed aged 25-30 without upper secondary education		Enrolling at the upper secondary level is not an obligation but is possible if they have been unemployed for a long period (typically more than 15 months)

Age over 30

General rule: Have to be activated after nine months of unemployment for a period of at least four weeks

Specific rule: Unemployment insurance recipients aged 60 and more have to be activated after six months of unemployment

Source: Danish Ministry of Employment.

Intensified intervention in the crisis

In November 2009, a series of policies designed to ensure a quick, intensive and focused approach towards youth aged 18-29 have been decided to be implemented immediately by the PES. These actions cover both the Ministry of Education and the Ministry of Employment.

First, measures targeted at the 18-19-year-olds are based on intensive contact and rapid activation. An immediate offer will be provided for unemployed between 18 and 19 years consisting of an individual talk after only one week of unemployment, a clarifying course within the first two weeks and an active offer (an educational opportunity or work placement by the local council) no later than one month after the beginning of their unemployment period.

Second, other initiatives are targeted at the 18-30-year-olds. Among them, there are the following:

- Young people under 30, who have been recipients of public benefits for longer than 12 months, will be eligible for a special subsidy provided by the PES to receive active offers in the private sector.

- Young people without qualifications will be able to take a reading and writing test when they become unemployed, and job centres have been given resources to provide literacy and numeracy courses.

- Newly graduated students under 30 will be obliged to be referred by the PES to a private provider after only six weeks of unemployment. Previously new graduates were passed on after 4-7 months depending on their educational attainment. The new accelerated process should prevent long-term unemployment among them.

D. Monitoring and evaluation of youth activation

Only 5% of newly unemployed youth had to be activated in 2007

With generous benefits and high income tax rates (already at fairly low levels of earnings), Denmark supposedly faces a high risk of unemployment traps among young people. However, in 2007, less than 5% of unemployed young people who were receiving unemployment benefits stayed unemployed longer than six months (Table 4.2) and consequently started an action plan. This achievement can be, at least partially, ascribed to Denmark's well-designed activation measures targeted at youth that successfully promote a rapid reintegration in employment.

Evaluations of activation programmes for youth: back to education or reintegration into employment?

Jensen *et al.* (2003) find that the 1996 enacted Youth Unemployment Programme (YUP) had a clear positive effect on the transition rate into education, whereas the effect on transition into employment was more uncertain. This means that the 1996 reform probably had more of an impact on the number of unemployment youth than on the youth unemployment rate.[68] Figure 4.5 indeed suggests that the decline in the Danish youth unemployment rate began in 1993. During the same period, the overall unemployment rate also receded markedly.

---

68. By definition, an unemployment rate is a ratio that can be affected by changes of both its numerator (the number of unemployed) and denominator (the number of individuals who participate to the labour force). When unemployed youth find a job the ratio unambiguously goes down. But when they return to education, the direction of the ratio is hard to predict as both the numerator and the denominator decline.

Table 4.2.   **Activation of young people, Denmark, 2004-07**

Numbers and percentages

	2004	2005	2006	2007
Number of recently unemployed youth[a] (A)	46 232	39 022	31 688	19 737
Number of recently unemployed youth who are still unemployed after six months[b] (B)	3 036	2 411	1 802	959
Number of recently unemployed youth who have obtained an action plan within six months of unemployment (C)	1 629	891	1 716	959
Share B/A (%)	6.6	6.2	5.7	4.9
Share C/A (%)	3.5	2.3	5.4	4.9

a) Data are based on the unemployment insurance funds' reporting of the unemployed persons first day of unemployment.

b) Data refer to the number of young unemployed persons with 26 weeks continuous full unemployment/re-training from the time of the first day of unemployment.

Source: Danish Government (2008), *Denmark's National Reform Programme: Contribution to the EU's Growth and Employment Strategy (the Lisbon Strategy).*

Figure 4.5.   **Adult[a] and youth[b] percentage unemployment rates, Denmark, 1990-2008**

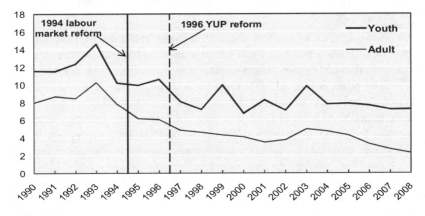

a) Aged 15-24.
b) Aged 25-54.
Source: OECD Labour Force database.

Jensen *et al.* (2003), using Danish monthly unemployment data, argue that the decline in adult unemployment is actually smaller than the decline in youth unemployment, and the gap between youth and overall unemployment rates became noticeably wider after the implementation of YUP in April 1996. They further state that it is difficult to know whether this pattern is due to YUP or is simply a consequence of youth unemployment being more cyclically sensitive than the aggregate unemployment rate and consequently decreasing faster during booming periods – something supported by the analysis of how the youth unemployment rate responds to the business cycle presented in Chapter 3.

Evaluations of activation programmes for youth: threat versus programme effect?

Even in the 1980s and the early 1990s, when unemployment rates were persistently high, the two components of the Danish *flexicurity* model (Box 3.1) were already in place in the Danish labour market, but the active labour market policy was not as intensive as today. Therefore, many observers see intensive activation policies as a pivotal component in the *flexicurity* model's achievement (Rosholm, 2008; Zhou, 2007).

But activation policies are costly both in terms of administration and programme costs. Given the extensive use of these policies in Denmark, it is not surprising that public expenditure in PES and administration and in ALMPs are among the highest in the OECD area, constituting respectively 0.28% and 1.02% of GDP in 2007 while the OECD average was 0.15% and 0.40% of GDP (OECD, 2009d). This raises the question of whether the effects of activation are worth the resources spent (Andersen and Svarer, 2007; Svarer, 2007).

Various studies stress that there is a clear evidence of strong threat effects of activation policies while the evidence on the programme effects[69] of individual ALMPs *per se* are mixed (see Rosholm, 2008; Kluve *et al.*, 2007). The point is that ALMPs form the expensive part of the scheme. In 2005-06, there was an interesting experimental evaluation to assess the effectiveness of ALMPs in Denmark (Box 4.1). The main findings were that there was a significant positive effect on the outflow from unemployment to employment and that this effect was generated mostly by the perceived risk of: *i)* intensified monitoring and programme participation; and/or *ii)* benefit cuts associated to participation (*i.e.* the threat). There is also some empirical evidence that job search by unemployed persons is intensified just prior to enrolment in ALMPs. In addition, people who receive benefits but have little or no interest in being available for work typically leave the unemployment insurance system when they are required to participate in ALMPs (Danish Economic Council, 2002).

---

69. The threat effect is the increase in search effort brought about by the threat of having to participate in ALMPs. The programme effect is the expected positive implications for the chances of an unemployed person finding a job due to the training or experience they have received while participating in an ALMP.

Box 4.1. **The Danish experiment on early intervention and intensive counselling for the newly unemployed in 2005-06**

A natural experiment in labour market policy was carried out in two counties in Denmark during the winter of 2005-06. Approximately 5 000 newly unemployed people participated in this pilot programme (European Employment Observatory, 2008).

The treatment consisted of increasing early intervention to unemployed people during the first weeks of their unemployment. This involves information, early mandatory participation in job search assistance programmes, frequent meetings with employment officers, and full-time programme participation for at least three months of people who had not found a job within 18 weeks of becoming unemployed.

In general, the results of this experiment showed that there was a significant positive effect on the outflow from unemployment to employment. Graversen and van Ours (2008) find that the job finding rate of unemployed persons in the treatment group is 30% higher than in the control group. The reduction in median unemployment duration is also higher, at 18%. The authors speculate that the threat effect as well as intensive monitoring and counselling, *i.e.* the stick rather than the carrot, might explain this strong treatment effects in Denmark. When divided into sub-periods, the effects were only significant during weeks 5-18 of the experiment, exactly the period when intervention was most intense, and ending with planned activation after about four months. The effects were greater for young unemployed people (<30) and for older unemployed people.

Rosholm (2008), also using the results of the experiment, finds that the intensification of labour market policies is highly effective, leading to increases in the exit rate from unemployment ranging from 20-40%, varying by region and elapsed unemployment duration. Meanwhile, the author finds that, while none of the various specific treatments prescribed to the participants (*e.g.* job search assistance, various meetings and programmes) have a positive effect on the exit rate from unemployment, the anticipated risk of participating in an activation programme in a given week has a strong positive effect on the job-finding rate (*i.e.*, individual treatments do not appear to be effective *per se*, but the perceived risk of treatment appears effective).

The Danish Economic Council (2007b) has conducted a cost-benefit analysis of the experimental intensification of active measures, using detailed cost information and calculating as benefits the reduction in unemployment benefit payments multiplied by the price of providing public funds (tax distortion) and the increased value of production resulting from reduced unemployment duration. They estimate the socio-economic value of the intensification about EUR 2 000 (DKK 15 000) per person. The social gain from the experiment is estimated after 46 weeks, and thus does not include the long-term effects.

The measures used in this experiment are now being disseminated to the PES nationwide through a campaign initiated by the Ministry of Employment in January 2008. The ministry also has launched a second-generation experiment, where the different tools and practices applied in early intervention are to be tested in more detail.

3. Active labour market programmes

A.   Denmark spent about 2.5% of its GDP on active and passive labour market programmes in 2007

Public expenditure in active and passive labour market programmes in Denmark is high by international standards. In 2007, Denmark spent 2.51% of its GDP on active and passive labour market policy (PES and administration excluded), the highest level after Belgium among European countries (Figure 4.6). However, Denmark, like other EU countries, spends more on passive measures (1.5% of GDP) – UIB and early retirement – than on active ones[70] (1.02% of GDP), the only exception being Sweden. However, the gap between active and passive measures has narrowed a lot in Denmark in the 1990s, and is the lowest in 2007 before the onset of the current economic crisis.

Figure 4.6.   **Labour market programme (LMP) expenditure,[a] selected European countries, 2007**

As a percentage of GDP

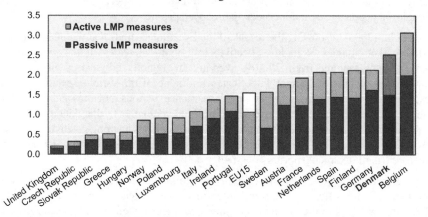

a)   Categories 2-7 (training, employment incentives, supported employment rehabilitation, direct job creation and starts-up incentives) are counted as active measures and categories 8-9 (out-of-work income maintenance and support and early retirement) as passive measures.

Source: Eurostat/OECD database on Labour Market Programmes.

---

70.   Categories 2-7 of the OECD-Eurostat classification: training, employment incentives, supported employment rehabilitation, direct job creation and starts-up incentives.

An interesting feature of Denmark's financing of labour market policy is that the national budget for ALMPs is adjusted according to the government's official unemployment forecasts. Hence, during recessions (like today's) sufficient funding is available to support the larger number of unemployed persons, including young individuals.

B.   *Main active labour market programmes (ALMPs)*

The Consolidated Act on Active Employment Measures of 2005 prescribes three main ALMPs: *i) guidance and upgrading of skills and qualifications; ii) practical work training in enterprises;* and *iii) wage subsidies.* These instruments can be combined according to the needs of the person and/or those of the labour market (Eurostat, 2009).

First, the *guidance and upgrading of skills and qualifications* programme has three basic instruments: "specially arranged activation", "short guidance and skills qualifying programmes" and "education and training". These instruments are normally used for a period of up to six weeks. However, they can be used for up to 26 weeks if learning the Danish language is a major part of activation measures and for up to one year in case, for example, the unemployed person has to acquire skills in sectors experiencing skill shortages. "Specially arranged activation" is implemented through, for example, information meetings, work experiences in enterprises, job seeking activities, recruitment interviews and job tests. The measure may also contain educational activities. "Short guidance and skills qualifying programmes" are carried out also through information meetings, job seeking activities, recruitment interviews and job tests. Activation in "education and training" includes training either in the general education/training system or in especially tailor-made programmes.

Second, *practical work training in enterprises* is to provide a practical work experiences for the hard-to-place group of the unemployed who are not immediately job-ready. Participants keep receiving their previous benefits, and are not employed in enterprises. This programme may be carried on at, for example, private associations, private households, sport clubs, cultural organisations as well as in the public sector. It lasts normally four weeks, but the authorities may prolong it up to 26 weeks according to the needs of the unemployed persons.

Third, *wage subsidies* are available both for private and public employers. To be eligible for the subsidy, the subsidised job should result in an increase in the number of staff in the firm and there should be a reasonable proportion between subsidised employment and ordinary employment within the firm. In the private sector according to collective agreements, wages and working conditions are the same for participants as for regular employees. In contrast, for participants in the public sector, monthly earnings equal unemployment insurance benefits (Jespersen *et al.*, 2008). This programme targets primarily the unemployed who is almost immediately ready for a normal job, but needs small adjustments in personal qualifications. This programme can be used for a period of up to one year. In case of private employers, subsidised employment is only available for an unemployed person who faces a special risk of long-term unemployment or has already been long-term unemployed for at least 12 months (six months in the case of the unemployed person under the age of 30) and has received social assistance benefits.

C.   *Youth programmes*

Until 2002, public expenditure on youth programmes[71] could be easily traced in the OECD database. In 2002, expenditure for youth programmes in Denmark came to 0.10% of GDP, slightly more than the OECD average (0.08% of GDP). From 2002 onwards, the Eurostat database no longer reports on public expenditure on youth programmes. Countries are just asked to say whether participants are aged less than 25. Unfortunately, only 16 countries responded and not for all the programmes.[72] On average in 2007 – for the 16 countries that filled in the age of participants – the proportion of participants represented 67% of unemployed youth, but only 29% in Denmark (Figure 4.7). This share is relatively low compared with countries like Italy, France and Austria where more than 90% of the unemployed youth participated in ALMPs. As discussed earlier, the Danish situation might be explained by the fact that a mere 5% of unemployed youth stayed unemployed for more than six months (see Table 4.2).

In 2007 in Denmark, training was the most widely attended programme by youth: 58% of participants aged less than 25 were in training programmes. Training is however less frequent than in Poland, Ireland, Germany, France and Austria where the proportion is more than 80%. Administrative data on ALMP participation show that the training programme called "specially adapted projects and educational activities" is particularly frequent among the unemployed aged 16-24, followed by job search assistance (guidance and clarification activities) (Table 4.3). The

---

71.   The OECD classification of youth measures included from 1995 to 2002 specific measures for unemployed youth and subsidies for apprenticeship and other types of general youth training. From 2002 onwards, the OECD database is derived from the Eurostat database.

72.   As the response rate differs by age group, programme and country, international comparison needs to be interpreted with caution.

unemployed aged 25-29 benefit first from adult apprenticeship support, followed by training programmes such as specially adapted projects and educational activities and ordinary education.

Figure 4.7.   **Youth ALMPs in selected European countries,[a] 2007[b]**

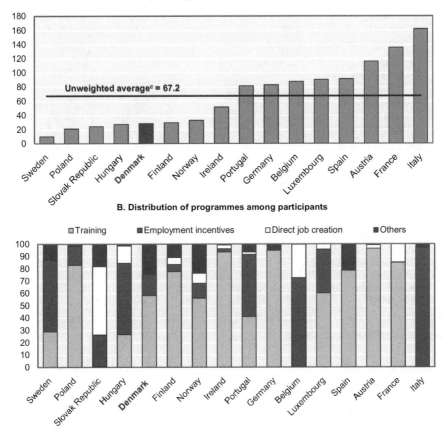

a)   Data on participants are not available for some ALMPs in the Eurostat database, thus making aggregate data not fully reliable. The aggregate data presented here refer to those which cover at least 80% of relevant expenditure.

b)   2003 for Spain; 2006 for Germany.

c)   Unweighted average of countries shown in the chart.

Source: Eurostat/OECD Labour Market Programmes database.

Table 4.3.   **Participants in active labour market programmes,[a] by age, Denmark, 2007**

Persons and percentages of registered unemployed persons by age

	All ages		Aged 16-24		Aged 25-29	
	Persons	Share	Persons	Share	Persons	Share
Registered unemployed persons	77 165	100.0	5 649	100.0	9 054	100.0
Guidance and upgrading of skills and qualifications	38 482	49.9	5 180	91.7	5 214	57.6
Guidance and clarification activities	9 046	11.7	1 443	25.5	1 086	12.0
Specially adapted projects and educational activities	16 302	21.1	3 126	55.3	2 328	25.7
Ordinary education	13 090	17.0	602	10.7	1 792	19.8
Special activities upgrading skills	44	0.1	10	0.2	8	0.1
Subsidised employment	73 943	95.8	1 848	32.7	6 857	75.7
Business in-service training	6 507	8.4	849	15.0	742	8.2
Employment subject to wage subsidies	7 882	10.2	431	7.6	877	9.7
Flex jobs	43 861	56.8	448	7.9	1 211	13.4
Sheltered jobs	4 902	6.4	118	2.1	336	3.7
Service jobs	705	0.9	0	0.0	0	0.0
Adult apprenticeship support	10 088	13.1	2	0.0	3 690	40.8
Integration education (Danish lessons)	1 928	2.5	208	3.7	479	5.3

a)   Data refer to the average number of participants in each labour market policy measure.
Source: Statistics Denmark, StatBank.

Beyond threat: the mixed programme/treatment effects of youth ALMPs

As mentioned earlier, while several studies confirm the "threat effects" of Danish activation policies, there is mixed evidence on the "programme effect" or "treatment effect" of individual ALMPs. Some even argue that the actual objective of ALMPs – to improve the job and wage prospects of the unemployed – has not been achieved (Danish Economic Council, 2002).

Kluve *et al.* (2007) have reviewed the recent evaluation studies on Danish ALMPs. In general, private sector employment programmes appear to have positive effects, whereas training programmes – which is the most widely used programme for youth in Denmark – and public sector employment programmes have negative effects, by prolonging unemployment duration, primarily *via* large negative locking-in effects.

The Danish Economic Council (2007b) also shows that some programmes have a negative effect on employment and earnings. On-the-job training in the private and public sectors are the only programmes displaying a positive effect on subsequent employment and earnings. Classroom training – that incidentally is mostly attended by individuals with a relatively high educational attainment – and other programmes have a negative effect of employment and wages. Cost-benefit evaluation of ALMPs shows a high deficit for classroom training, while on-the-job training in the private and the public sectors present a surplus. The Council recommends that classroom training should be more focused and targeted on those of the unemployed who can benefit from participation. It further recommends giving priority to counselling, job-search assistance and more systematic availability-for-work testing (Danish Economic Council, 2007b).

Research done by Jespersen *et al.* (2008) covering the years 1995 to 2005, largely accords with that of the Danish Economic Council. It also finds that job training in the private sector generates a high return, which is mainly due to substantially higher earnings and reduced income transfers after participation. Public job training also generates a significant value added while classroom training generates a significant deficit.

Which activation strategy for very disadvantaged youth?

Most of the 2000s were synonymous with low unemployment and skill shortages in Denmark. This means that a growing share of unemployed youth consisted of individuals intrinsically hard to place in employment, who for instance had a record of underachievement at school, of substance/alcohol addiction or mental illness. Traditional ALMPs – counselling, job-search assistance, training programme and even financial incentives – tend to prove ineffective at dealing with such a public.

The recent downturn may make such a public less visible among the inflated ranks of unemployed youth, removing some of the political pressure to address its needs. That said, in the future, in view of population ageing and other long-term trends, Denmark will probably anew be confronted with the problem of insufficient skilled labour to sustain growth. Therefore, Denmark will probably need to keep developing programmes with the capacity to reach out to very disadvantaged youth in order to reintegrate them into regular employment.

The Danish government recently introduced a programme called "4K" targeting youth with psychosocial disabilities (Box 4.2) associating municipalities with private employers.

Box 4.2. The "4K", a project for youth with psychosocial disabilities

The project "4K" was initiated by the Minister of Employment and Danish Disability Organisations with the support of the Danish National Network of Business. The name "4K" has two meanings. It involves at least four young people at the same time into a business centre, and the project is characterised by the following four points:

- *Candidate for employment and education*: the project provides the young people to get closer to the labour market and eventually hope to get an ordinary job.

- *Competences*: participants develop their personal and professional skills through participation in a business centre.

- *Social skills*: participants will have new social contacts with other young people in the business centre as well as colleagues at the company.

- *Contact mentor*: contact between the candidate and the mentor from the company is an important cornerstone in the project. The mentor helps and supports the candidate through the course at the workplace.

The target group for the project "4K" comprises young people under age 30 with psychosocial disabilities who receive social assistance (*i.e.* cash benefit) or other disadvantaged youth. The goal is to get the young people ready for employment or further education. The group includes a wide range of young people with psychosocial disabilities like ADHD (Attention-deficit hyperactivity disorder), brain damage, or with "an uneven start in life", such as young single mothers and third-generation cash-benefit recipient. The experiment is designed to prevent the target group from dropping out of the labour market before the age of 30.

Currently, there are two municipalities participating in "4K" alongside four private companies. Each company has set up an absorption centre, called a business centre. Hence, there are a total of 32 participants in this project. There can be awarded maximum EUR 4 000 (DKK 30 000) per participant. The grant is used partly to supplement or to subsidise Job centres and to support businesses and participants in the form of, such as, mentoring and physical education.

Among programmes targeted specifically to very disadvantaged youth, there is some experimental evidence that residential programmes with a strong focus on remedial learning and employment assistance may yield positive private and social returns once allowance is made for impacts on adverse social behaviours (crime, drug-taking, poor parenting), as well as labour market outcomes. An example of these programmes, the Job Corps in the United States, is presented in Box 4.3. This is however an expensive programme, costing more than USD 20 000 per participant. Although the evalution litterature has been very positive about the outcomes of this programme, a recent synthesis paper by Schochet *et al.* (2008) suggest that Job Corps is cost-effective is primarily for young adults (aged 20-24).

Box 4.3. **The US Job Corps programme**

For several decades, Job Corps has been a central part of the US Federal government's efforts to provide employment assistance to disadvantaged youth and help them become "more responsible, employable and productive citizens". To be eligible, youth must be 16-24, meet low-income criteria and face one or more barriers to employment such as lacking qualifications or being a runaway, a foster child, a teenage parent or a homeless youth. Job Corps services are delivered at 122 centres nationwide in the United States and serve about 60 000 new enrolees annually. Most youth participate in a campus-like residential living component – approximately 85% of students are residential – while the remaining students commute to their centres daily. Participation is entirely on a voluntary basis.

Programme components include a strong focus on academic education and vocational training to help participants attain an upper secondary qualification. Thanks to close cooperation with unions, some vocational training courses available at Job Corps are recognised as pre-apprenticeship programmes, allowing entry to apprenticeships at a higher level and salary. At the end of the programme lasting normally eight months, placement services help participants to secure sustainable employment. Other key services include health education, health care and counselling. During the programme, youth receive a stipend twice a month – increasing with seniority, up to USD 46 – and a lump sum of USD 100 every three months to purchase of technical-training clothing. Youth who complete vocation training and obtain an upper-secondary qualification are eligible for USD 1 200 to help with the start-up costs of independent life.

Outreach activities, centre management, training and placement services are all run by private contractors. Contracts are allocated through a competitive tendering process and can last up to seven years after a series of renewals. All contractors are evaluated based on several criteria each carrying a different weight, with some weights modelled on the characteristics of the population in each Job Corps centre. For instance, outreach contractors are evaluated based on: the number of youth recruited; the percentage of women recruited; the share of recruited youth who remain enrolled for a minimum of 60 days; and the share of recruited youth who do not separate within 30/45 days due to a violation of Job Corps' Zero Tolerance policy against violence/drugs. On the other hand, contractors who run the centres are evaluated based on: the share of participants who acquire an upper secondary qualification; the share of participants who complete vocational training; the literary and numeracy gains of participants; the initial placement of graduates; the match between a graduate placement and the training received at Job Corps; the initial placement of non-terminees (youth who do not acquire an upper secondary qualification while on the programme); the initial graduate wage; the employment status of a graduate six months after exit; the graduate wage six months after exit; and the employment status of a graduate 12 months after exit. The achievement of these goals influences contractors' payment in the form of extra bonus payments – *i.e.* centre contractors are only allowed to bid for costs and a profit margin of 2.8% but can attain profits of up to 6% if they perform well according to the above-mentioned criteria.

Job Corps is an expensive programme given its design, costing approximately USD 22 000 per participant (OECD, 2009g). As a result, it has been evaluated several times during its history, most recently *via* experimental (*i.e.* random-assignment) methods. Schochet *et al.* (2001) found rather positive effects of Job Corps on participants' employability and earnings and high social rates of return. However, a follow-up analysis based on administrative data on earnings rather than survey-based data (Schochet *et al.*, 2003) found less positive benefits for teenagers but continued to show high social returns for young adults (the 20-24 age group). The residential component of the programme appears to work better than the non-residential option.

4. Public and private employment services

The proportion of unemployed youth who register with the PES in Denmark is relatively low among OECD countries (Figure 4.8). Part of the explanation might be the division of the role between the PES (in charge of unemployment benefit) and the municipal authorities (in charge of social assistance) which existed until very recently. From the summer of 2009, the PES has been further decentralised and all unemployed persons, irrespective of their benefit level, will be dealt with by the zone agency (one-stop shop) in each municipality.

Figure 4.8.   **Unemployed youth registered with the PES, 2006-07[a]**

As a percentage of unemployed aged 15-24

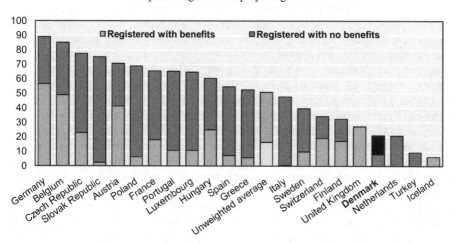

a)   Data refer to a 2006 and 2007 average.

Source: Estimations based on the European Union Labour Force Survey (EULFS).

A.   *Towards one-stop shops at the municipal level*

Until the summer of 2009, there were two different ALMP delivering systems: the central state system (the Ministry of Employment) that dealt with the members of the unemployment insurance funds and the municipal system that dealt with recipients of social benefits (Winter *et al.*, 2008).

From 2007, the access point for these two groups of beneficiaries was different. The local government reform in 2007 introduced a new administrative structure for employment policy. The central and local government provision of employment services were merged into jointly-functioning new PES (job centres) located at the municipal level.[73]

The 91 local job centres, which are staffed by both local and central government employees, have become a single access point for all citizens and companies needing assistance in employment matters. Furthermore, on a pilot basis, seven job centres are run entirely by the local government without central government involvement – *i.e.* the municipalities took over the state's responsibility for the unemployed with insurance.

The new approach creates a greater focus on employment by removing the distinction in employment services based on the kind of income support the unemployed person receives (OECD, 2008e).

Recently, the government decided to move forwards by completely merging the two systems in order to provide exactly the same offers and conditions for all unemployed irrespective of whether they are insured or not. Therefore all job centres are run by the municipal authorities from August 2009.

With this reform, some concerns have been raised by the social partners as well as some researchers. First, there might be a risk of fragmentation of labour market intermediation and the municipal focus may hinder labour mobility by focusing the unemployed and jobs within the municipality (OECD, 2008e). In addition, Winter *et al.* (2008) find that in Denmark the central provision of services is more consistent with national policy goals than the local provision of national policies. Second, there is a risk of heterogeneity in the way the activation process is implemented among different municipalities.

---

73.   The 2007 structural reform reduced the number of municipalities from 271 to 98 municipalities.

However, these risks can be counterbalanced by: *i)* the detailed regulations imposed by central authorities as to how municipalities should treat their clients; and *ii)* state-of-art benchmarking capabilities by municipality, such as *Jobindsats.*[74]

B.   Towards a coherent guidance system

There are no specialised public employment agencies targeting youth in Denmark. However, in recent years, the government established youth guidance centres to provide educational and vocational guidance to school drop-outs (see Section 5, Chapter 2 and Box 4.4).

C.   Co-operation between private and public employment agencies

In 1990, the PES monopoly on placement services was abolished in Denmark. Since 2003, part of employment services has been outsourced to private agencies, including trade unions. An average of around 30% of unemployed people was referred to other actors than the PES in 2004, while the minimum legal obligation for outsourcing is 10%. Preliminary evaluation studies show that private agencies perform marginally better than the PES in helping the unemployed to return to work (Dingeldey, 2007, quoting Bredgaard *et al.*, 2005). Greater outsourcing and privatisation of employment services are being pursued in conjunction with the 2007 Reform on local government and employment services (Dingeldey, 2007).

In case of temporary agency work, the share of temporary agency workers among total employment in Denmark was one of the lowest in Europe, although this share has increased in recent years, from 0.3% in 1999 to 0.9% in 2006 (Bredgaard *et al.*, 2009). This situation might be explained by the fact that there is no legal provision for temporary agency work in Denmark, and so this type of employment is regulated only through collective agreements.

---

74.   *Jobindsats.dk* is an Internet portal which provides information and data on the latest results of the employment policy programmes. *Jobindsats.dk* offers a large selection of data *e.g.* on the developments in youth unemployment. *Jobindsats.dk* makes it possible to closely monitor the developments in employment policy at local level, and serves as an efficient tool for central and local government as well as researchers. It is possible to perform searches on a wide range of variables, including geographical areas, periods, gender, ethnic background, age and match category.

Box 4.4. **Youth guidance centres in Denmark**

There are 45 municipal youth guidance centres to provide guidance services for young people up to the age of 25 years. The youth guidance centres focus on guidance related to the transition from compulsory school to youth education or, alternatively, to the labour market. The main target groups are:

- Pupils in primary and lower secondary school – forms 6 to 9 (10)

- Young people under the age of 25 who are not involved in education, training or employment. The centres provide outreach services for this group as they are obliged to establish contact with these young people and help them get back into education and training or employment.

- Other young people under the age of 25 who contact the centres themselves for guidance.

- Young people with a special need for guidance – a transversal target group that includes young people whose problems are related to the continuing or completion of an education programme.

Guidance activities include individual and group guidance sessions, as well as introductory courses and bridge building schemes to give pupils a "taste" of conditions, levels and requirements at different youth education institutions.

Cross-sectoral co-operation is emphasised in the Danish legislation on guidance to ensure a coherent guidance system and a regular exchange of experiences, knowledge and best practice. The youth guidance centres are thus obliged to co-operate closely with the PES (job centres) as well as primary and secondary schools and youth education institutions in the area.

Source: Danish Ministry of Education; *www.uvm.dk/*.

---

5. Key points

Unemployed young people in Denmark are covered by one of the most generous income-support system in the OECD area. The net replacement rate provided by unemployment insurance benefits is among the highest in OECD, and the maximum benefit duration of four years is also one of the longest. Means-tested social assistance is also generous by international standards and available for all those who do not (or no longer) qualify for unemployment insurance benefits as from the age of 18.

While relatively generous welfare schemes theoretically bear the risk of creating unemployment and inactivity traps, in Denmark activation measures targeted at youth successfully promote their rapid reintegration in employment. This is a result of a strict and well-established implementation of the "mutual obligations" activation approach introduced in the mid-1990s whereby, in exchange for income support, job seekers (including youth) need to participate in training, job-search or placement activities (the flexicurity approach).

During the second part of the 1990s and in the early 2000s, activation was fine-tuned and reinforced, especially in relation to youth, with apparent success. Today, early intervention is considered as the fastest way to bring people back to work. The benefit is reduced for youth under 25 (without children) after six months of activation. From the summer 2009, after a first job interview within one month of unemployment and a maximum of three months of unemployment, all unemployed youth less than 30 must take part in activation programmes. However, activation rules are the strictest for youth under the age of 25 without an upper secondary qualification and without children. They are obliged to enter an education programme, either in the ordinary educational system if they are ready for taking on education or otherwise in a special education programme to make them ready to enter the ordinary educational system. By contrast, all types of ALMPs can be proposed to youth aged 25-29 and for youth with children.

Many analysts see intensive activation policies as a pivotal component of Denmark's good labour market performances. Various studies confirm the strong "threat effect" of Danish activation policies, while the evidence on the effect of individual programmes is mixed. In other words, what works is the perceived risk of treatments (and the string of financial sanctions attached to them), not the (relatively expensive) treatments.

BIBLIOGRAPHY

Andersen, T. and M. Svarer (2007), "Flexicurity – Labour Market Performance in Denmark", School of Economics and Management Economics Working Paper, No. 2007-9, University of Aarhus.

Blanchflower, D.G. and R. Freeman (1996), "Growing into Work", Paper presented at the NBER Conference on Youth Unemployment and Employment in Advanced Countries, December 12-14, Winston-Salem.

Boocock, S. (1995), "Early Childhood Programmes in Other Countries: Goals and Outcomes", *The Future Children,* Vol. 5, No. 3, Los Altos, California.

Bredgaard, T. and F. Larsen (eds.) (2005), *Employment Policy from Different Angles*, Danish Association of Lawyers and Economists (DJøF), Copenhagen.

Bredgaard, T. and F. Larsen (2007), *Comparing Flexicurity in Denmark and Japan*, Centre for Labour Market Research at Aalborg University (CARMA), Denmark.

Bredgaard, T., F. Larsen, per K. Madsen and S. Rasmussen (2009), "Flexicurity and Atypical Employment in Denmark", CARMA Research Paper, 2009-01, Aalborg University.

Caille, J.P. and F. Rosenwald (2006), "Les inégalités de réussite à l'école élémentaire : construction et evolution", *France : Portrait Social*, Institut National de la Statistique et des Études Économiques (INSEE), Paris.

Carneiro, P. and J. Heckman (2003), "Human Capital Policy", IZA Discussion Paper, No. 821, Bonn.

Danish Economic Council (2002), *The Danish Economy* (English Summary), Copenhagen.

Danish Economic Council (2007a), *A Long-Term Projection of the Danish Economy. The Role of Immigration for the Labour Force. Integration of Immigrants and their Offspring*, Copenhagen.

Danish Economic Council (2007b), *Business Cycles and Fiscal Policy. Danish Labour Market Policy since 2000*, Copenhagen.

Danish Government (2008), *Denmark's National Reform Programme: Contribution to the EU's Growth and Employment Strategy (The Lisbon Strategy)*, Copenhagen.

Danish Ministry of Education (2008), *Facts and Figures 2007. Key Figures in Education 2007*, Statistical Publication, No. 3, Copenhagen.

Danish Ministry of Finance (2006), *Denmark's Convergence Programme 2006*, November, Copenhagen.

Dansk Arbejdsgiverforening (2009), *Arbejdsmarkedsrapport 2009*, Copenhagen.

Deding, M. and M. Larsen (2008), *Mænd Lønforskelle mellem mænd og kvinder 1997-2006*, Socialforskningsinstituttet (SFI), Report No. 191 s, Copenhagen.

Dingeldey, I. (2007), "Between Workfare and Enablement – The Different Paths to Transformation of the Welfare State: a Comparative Analysis of Activating Labour Market Policies", *European Journal of Political Research*, Vol. 46, No. 6, pp. 823-851.

Eckstein, Z. and K.I. Wolpin (1999), "Why Youths Drop out of High School: the Impact of Preferences, Opportunities, and Abilities", *Econometrica*, No. 67, pp. 1295-1340.

European Employment Observatory (2008), *EEO Review: Spring 2008 – Innovative Labour Market Policies and Practices*, European Employment Observatory, Brussels.

Eurostat (2009), *Labour Market Policy Qualitative Report – Denmark 2007*, Statistical Office of the European Communities, Working Papers and Studies, Luxemburg.

Eurydice (2007), *Key Data on Higher Education in Europe*, Brussels.

Geerdsen, L.P. and A. Holm (2007), "Duration of UI Periods and the Perceived Threat Effect from Labour Market Programmes", *Labour Economics*, Vol. 14, No. 3, pp. 639-652.

Graversen, B.K. and J.C. van Ours (2008), "How To Help Unemployed Find Jobs Quickly: Experimental Evidence from a Mandatory Activation Programme", *Journal of Public Economics*, Vol. 92, No. 10-11, pp. 2020-2035.

Greenberger, E. and L.D. Steinberg (1986), *The Psychological and Social Costs of Adolescent Employment*, Basic, New York.

Gupta, N. and M. An (2005), "The Effect of Labour Market Conditions on the Completion of Higher Education in Denmark", *Danish Journal of Economics*, Vol. 143, No. 1, pp. 81-103.

Hodrick, R.J. and E.C. Prescott (1997), "Postwar U.S. Business Cycles: An Empirical Investigation", *Journal of Money, Credit and Banking*, Vol. 29, No. 1, pp. 1-16.

Jensen, P., M. Rosholm and M. Svarer (2003), "The Response of Youth Unemployment to Benefits, Incentives, and Sanctions", *European Journal of Political Economy*, Vol. 19, No. 2, pp. 301-316.

Jespersen, S.T., J.R. Munch and L. Skipper (2008), "Costs and Benefits of Danish Active Labour Market Programmes", *Labour Economics*, Vol. 15, No. 5, pp. 859-884.

Jørgensen, C. (2006), "Low Level of Membership by Young People in Unemployment Insurance Funds", European Industrial Relations Observatory, *www.eurofound.europa.eu/eiro/2006/10/articles/dk0610039i.htm*

Kluve, J., D. Card, M. Fertig, M. Gora, L. Jacobi, P. Jensen, R. Leetmaa, L. Nima, E. Patacchini, S. Schaffner, C.M. Schmidt, B. van der Klaauw and A. Weber (2007), *Active Labour Market Policies in Europe: Performance and Perspectives*, Springer, Berlin.

Labour Market Commission (2009), *Velfærd kræver arbejde*, August, Copenhagen.

Lefèbvre, P., P. Merrigan and M. Verstraete (2006), "Impact of Early Childhood Care and Education on Children's Preschool Cognitive Development: Canadian Results from a Large Scale Quasi-Experiment", Centre interuniversitaire sur le risque, les politiques économiques et l'emploi (CIRPÉE), Working Paper No. 06-36, Montréal.

Leschke, J. (2007), "Are Unemployment Insurance Systems in Europe Adapting to New Risks Arising from Non-standard Employment?", DULBEA Working Paper, No. 07-05.RS, Département d'Économie Appliquée de l'Université Libre de Bruxelles.

Liebig, T. (2007), "The Labour Market Integration of Immigrants in Denmark", OECD Social, Employment and Migration Working Paper, No. 50, OECD Publishing, Paris.

Liebig, T. and S. Widmaier, (2009), "Children of Immigrants in the Labour Markets of EU and OECD Countries: An Overview", OECD Social, Employment and Migration Working Paper, No. 97, OECD Publishing, Paris.

Moser, J.W. (1986), "Demographic and Time Patterns in Layoffs and Quits", *Journal of Human Resources*, Vol. 21, pp. 178-199.

National Education Authority (2008), *The Danish Vocational Education and Training System*, 2nd edition, Danish Ministry of Education, Copenhagen.

OECD (1999), *Preparing Youth for the 21st Century*, Proceedings of the Washington D.C. Conference, 21-23 February, OECD Publishing, Paris.

OECD (2004a), *Career Guidance and Public Policy. Bridging the Gap*, OECD Publishing, Paris.

OECD (2004b), *OECD Employment Outlook*, OECD Publishing, Paris.

OECD (2005a), *Ageing and Employment Policies: Denmark*, OECD Publishing, Paris.

OECD (2005b), "University Education in Denmark", *Review of National Policies for Education*, OECD Publishing, Paris.

OECD (2006a), *Starting Strong II: Early Childhood Education and Care*, OECD Publishing, Paris.

OECD (2006b), *OECD Economic Surveys: Denmark*, OECD Publishing, Paris.

OECD (2007), *Jobs for Immigrants. Vol. 1: Labour Market Integration in Australia, Denmark, Germany and Sweden*, OECD Publishing, Paris.

OECD (2008a), *Jobs for Youth/Des emplois pour les jeunes: Norway*, OECD Publishing, Paris.

OECD (2008b), *Jobs for Youth/Des emplois pour les jeunes: Canada*, OECD Publishing, Paris.

OECD (2008c), *OECD Employment Outlook*, OECD Publishing, Paris.

OECD (2008d), *Sickness, Disability and Work: Breaking the Barriers Vol. 3: Denmark, Finland, Ireland and the Netherlands*, OECD Publishing, Paris.

OECD (2008e), *OECD Economic Surveys: Denmark*, OECD Publishing, Paris.

OECD (2009a), *Education at a Glance*, OECD Publishing, Paris.

OECD (2009b), *Jobs for Youth/Des emplois pour les jeunes: Australia*, OECD Publishing, Paris.

OECD (2009c), "Sickness, Disability and Work: Keeping on Track in the EconomicDdownturn", Background Paper, High-Level Forum on Sickness, Disability and Work, organised jointly by the OECD and the

Government of Sweden, Stockholm, 15 May 2009, OECD Publishing, Paris.

OECD (2009d), *OECD Employment Outlook,* OECD Publishing, Paris.

OECD (2009e), *International Migration Outlook,* OECD Publishing, Paris.

OECD (2009f), *OECD Economic Surveys: Denmark*, OECD Publishing, Paris.

OECD (2009g), *Jobs for Youth/Des emplois pour les jeunes: United States*, OECD Publishing, Paris.

Oettinger, G. (1999), "Does High School Employment Affect High School Academic Performance?", *Industrial and Labor Relations Review,* Vol. 53, No. 1, pp. 136-151.

O'Higgins, N. (1997), "The Challenge of Youth Unemployment", Employment and Training Papers, No. 7, ILO, Geneva.

Patrinos, H.A. (2001), "School Choice in Denmark", mimeo, World Bank, Washington.

Rosholm, M. (2008), "Experimental Evidence on the Nature of the Danish Employment Miracle", IZA Discussion Paper, No. 3620, Bonn.

Ruhm, C. J. (1997), "Is High School Employment Consumption or Investment?", *Journal of Labor Economics*, Vol. 15, pp. 735-776.

Ryan, P. (1999), *The School-to-Work Transition: Issues for Further Investigation*, University of Cambridge, prepared for the Education and Training Division (DEELSA), OECD Publishing, Paris.

Schochet, P., J. Brughardt and S. Glazerman (2001), *National Job Corps Study: The Impacts of Job Corps on Participants' Employment and Related Outcomes,* Mathematica Policy Research, Inc., Princeton, New Jersey.

Schochet P., J. Burghardt and S. McConnell (2003), *National Job Corps Study: Findings Using Administrative Earnings Records Data*, Mathematica Policy Research, Inc., Princeton, New Jersey.

Schochet, P., J. Burgardt and S. McConnel (2008), "Does Job Corps Work? Impact Findings from the National Job Corps Study", *American Economic Review,* Vol. 98, No. 5, pp.1864-1886.

Svarer, M. (2007), "The Effect of Sanctions on the Job Finding Rate: Evidence from Denmark", IZA Discussion Paper, No. 3015, Bonn.

Swedish Fiscal Policy Council (2009), *Svensk finanspolitik 2009* [Swedish Fiscal Policy 2009], Stockholm.

Wandall, J. (2009), "National Tests in Denmark – CAT as a Pedagogic Tool", in F. Scheuermann & J. Björnsson (eds.), *New Approaches to Skills Assessment and Implications for Large-scale Testing, The Transition to Computer-Based Assessment,* Joint Research Centre Institute for the Protection and Security of the Citizen, European Commission, Brussels.

Westergaard-Nielsen, N. (2006), "Decentralised Wage Setting in Denmark after 1993?", Department of Economics and Center for Corporate Performance, Aarhus School of Business, EALE Conference 2006 Papers.

Winter, S.C., P.T. Dinesen and P.J. May (2008), "Implementation Regimes and Street-level Bureaucrats: Employment Service Delivery in Denmark", The Danish National Centre for Social Research, Working Paper No. 12:2008.

Zhou, J. (2007), "Danish for All? Balancing Flexibility with Security: the Flexicurity Model", IMF Working Paper, WP/07/36, International Monetary Fund, Washington.

OECD PUBLISHING, 2, rue André-Pascal, 75775 PARIS CEDEX 16
PRINTED IN FRANCE
(81 2010 04 1 P) ISBN 978-92-64-07515-3 – No. 57221 2010